HOOKED ON SCOTLAND

HOOKED
On Scotland

EDITED BY PAUL YOUNG

MAINSTREAM
PUBLISHING

EDINBURGH AND LONDON

in conjunction with

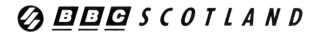

First published in Great Britain 1992 by
MAINSTREAM PUBLISHING COMPANY (EDINBURGH) LTD
7 Albany Street
Edinburgh EH1 3UG

ISBN 1 85158 433 1

A catalogue record for this book is available
from the British Library

Typeset in Palatino by Keyboard Services, Luton
Printed in Great Britain by Butler & Tanner Ltd, Frome, Somerset
Designed by Blue Peach, Glasgow

CONTENTS

INTRODUCTION

Paul Young

I have always thought that fishing was a bit like kissing – great fun to do but not the world's greatest spectator sport. Like fishing, you can enjoy kissing intensely. The heat of the moment can be deeply thrilling but, if you are not doing it yourself, it can leave you cold.

Taking the kissing metaphor a bit further, when you experience that first tingling kiss, it can lead to a commitment that can alter your whole life – in much the same way that catching your first trout, salmon or sea trout can. You start out knowing little more than the basic principles but eventually find that pleasure is to be derived in many different ways.

I have to say that I started fishing long before I started kissing, but with each one I was hooked from the start and have derived a great deal of fun from both over the years. I've even won cups and medals and was Scottish National Champion at one point – but unfortunately that was just at the fishing!

When I was first asked to present *Hooked on Scotland* it was realised that the series would have to communicate the pleasure and passion of fishing to anglers and, even more important to success, non-anglers alike. The programmes would have to be sufficiently interesting visually and scintillating enough in content for those who fish regularly, as well as capturing the attention of those who know little about the sport.

Angling is a highly popular participation sport with many different facets and nuances and our first problem was how to communicate these subtleties and delights successfully to other anglers – far less to the non-angling viewer. How do you convey the thrill of seeing a red-topped pike float slide gently underwater or, on a Highland river in summer, a grilse boil at the fly several times, just under the surface without actually touching it or a tope take a fresh mackerel bait with a searing 80-yard run? But then, most folk in Scotland have fished at some time in their lives. Off the pier on holiday for poodlies or with a worm in a spate-filled burn for troutlets or by taking string after string of mackerel on makeshift flies on an evening boat trip out from their holiday resort. So, it was reckoned, there might just possibly be a slightly wider potential audience than was first thought.

At least that was the theory put before BBC Scotland's Head of Television, Jim Hunter, and to his credit he agreed. There were to be eight programmes made, and the team would be Ricky Walker of Fairline Video as producer, Mike Shepley as director and myself as presenter.

We started filming on the River Tay at Kenmore on 15 January 1990 – the opening day of rod fishing for salmon on that great river. In fact, some northern rivers like the Helmsdale and the Thurso open a few days earlier but, with that touch of southern bias, the 15th is usually taken as 'the start'. We then filmed on and off until the end of October, when I had to go to London to fulfil a commitment to record a comedy series for Thames Television.

We travelled the country from Shetland to Luce Bay, and from Lewis to Kelso. We got soaked, we basked in the sunshine and we tried to catch fish in unlikely and interesting places throughout one of Scotland's uncharacteristically dry summers. But we did catch fish and I was lucky enough to sneak the odd one or two from waters with which I was totally unfamiliar.

It was an adventure from start to finish and because of

the vicissitudes of the Scottish weather we seldom knew where we would be filming, who we would meet or what we might catch. Too much sunshine was bad for fishing, and when it was wet and windy it made things either awkward, difficult or downright impossible technically. Just occasionally, though, we would be in the right place at the right time and something surprising and entertaining that showed the distinctiveness of Scottish angling would be safely captured on videotape. When the first episode of the series – on salmon fishing – was shown in early April 1991, I was somewhat surprised by the reaction. I know anglers love watching fishing programmes – sometimes if only to criticise kindly (I do it myself!) – but most fishers seemed to have genuinely enjoyed it. Indeed, more surprising still was the conspicuous pleasure of the non-anglers, hinting that we might just have got the formula right.

The eight programmes were based on species and techniques of fishing in Scotland. Salmon, sea trout, brown trout, rainbow trout and coarse fishing were the obvious freshwater choices and, with many species of sea fish in Scottish waters, we settled for shore, inshore and deep sea to represent saltwater fishing. We deliberately did not try to preach to people that *this* was the way to fish, *that* was the best place to go or that there was no *other* fly to fish than a *Dunkeld* or a *Wickham's Fancy*. We simply tried to capture and distil the spirit of fishing in Scotland.

I was hugely privileged to fish in places that not every angler will get to and some of the catches and incidents will live with me forever. Out from Tobermory on Mull with the Swinbanks brothers I caught my first-ever skate. It weighed 140 pounds – beating my previous best fish by 121½ pounds – took me nearly fifty minutes to land and was tagged and returned to the water alive. The same day we saw minke whales moving through the channel between Mull and Coll. One of them came out of the water and landed with a huge plume of salty spray. That day is firmly etched on my brain.

But my overall impression was of the characters we met. To a person they were warm and welcoming, kind and humorous and willing to share their thoughts, techniques, expertise and anecdotes with us and so with the viewer.

They have our grateful thanks.

As do the writers of the following chapters, many of whom took part in the series in one way or another. In this book they are giving individual perceptions of their particular branches of this wonderful sport and, like *Hooked on Scotland*, these essays from the heart are not really to tell you how to do it (though there are some helpful hints!), but more to entertain, to inform and to tell you why *they* do it.

I was also asked to tell you a bit about my own fishing life and hope that the tales of the hatching of an embryonic angler to the (possibly) mature specimen may be of some interest. Well, at my advanced stage in life, I'm now unfortunately better qualified to talk about the fishing than the kissing!

FIRST CASTS

Paul Young

I think I first became aware of fish, specifically trout, when I was nine years old and filming *Geordie* in the Trossachs. I was standing by the shore of Loch Katrine on a flat calm evening watching ever-expanding circles on the surface. I wondered what was happening when an angler hove into view, casting as he walked. He paused, not wading in, saw a fish rise and cast a dry fly on to the water in the vicinity of the rising fish and waited. I could see the little concoction of fur and feather sitting proudly on the smooth surface. He gave the line a tweak and the fly inched shorewards. As if in slow motion the neb, dorsal and tail of a fish lazily showed, the fly was taken and the angler hooked it. A shower of spray erupted as the fish cleared the water, the reel screeched as line was drawn . . . and the fish was off. The angler reeled in and as he passed me, blowing on the fly to dry it for the next cast, he said: 'That was good fun, eh?'

I thought it looked *brilliant* fun and fancied trying it myself. But where to start? I had no brothers or sisters to help, no tackle and no expertise, but there were relations who fished and I was determined.

As a family living in Edinburgh in the late '50s, we often used to go on a 'run' at the weekend. The car was a novelty to us and come Saturday or Sunday we would head for the

Borders. My mother, her sister and brother very proudly came from Galashiels and the A7 was like a magnet – 'the Golden Road to Gala' my mother called it – and quite often my grandparents would come with us on our weekend outings.

My grandfather was at this time chauffeur to Lord Rosebery and lived in one of the lodge cottages on Dalmeny estate near South Queensferry. He was no mean fisher himself and held me spellbound as he regaled me with stories of his own fishing trips. He was from Nisbet near Kelso, and the Teviot was on his doorstep. Nearby there was a pond covered with lily pads which was stuffed with perch and according to him they were monsters. With a glint in his eye he would put his left index finger in the crook of his right elbow, extend the fingers of his right hand and swear that the pond contained 'perches as lang as yer airm'.

He also told me of the time in the north somewhere when he and his companion were fishing a burn in the hills which suddenly disappeared. They followed what they thought was its course and came upon a hole in the ground. They could hear the sound of running water, so he slowly lowered a worm into the hole. A trout took immediately. As did many others and 'a' oot o' a hole in the grun'.

He also told of his long hike to Loch Einig where, at the mouth of a burn flowing into the loch, he took 'seeven and-a-half dizzen o' troots withoot moving frae the same spot', and, as if to answer my sceptical look, my grandmother confirmed the fact by saying, 'Aye, and I had tae clean the lot o' them!'

Perhaps it was from him that I caught the fishing bug.

We would often take a picnic and, if the call of Galashiels and the Golden Road was not too strong, we might head for Lauder or Eddleston. These outings invariably finished up by the waterside. We'd park near a handy bridge over a small burn, find some flat ground to sit on and I'd be off to explore. I was, and still am, fascinated by water. I used to spend hours dottering about by a burn and sometimes on these forays I'd see a dark shape rocket from the shallows to the safety of the deeper water and a rock at the head of a pool. One day I saw what must have been the carcase of a kelt. The skeleton was bare, the crows and gulls had removed the eyes and time and other predators had removed the flesh, but, like a Korky the Kat fish, there was the head, backbone and tail. I could not believe that fish so big existed and gleefully ran back with it to the rest of the picnickers to tell them of my great discovery. They were completely underwhelmed with the prospect of a fairly pongy corpse being waved under their noses and I was told in no uncertain terms to 'chuck that smelly thing away'. It probably weighed about four or five pounds, but I was hooked. If fish that size existed, I wanted to catch them.

Sometimes, though, the call of Galashiels was too strong and the Morris Minor, SSG 729, would be off on the Route d'Or. My uncle Hendy lived on the Melrose Road and he would often take me down to Tweedside. Gala Water joined its mother river close by and Hendy would talk of the 'evening rise'. This was a new phenomenon to me and I watched entranced as his tiny Tupp's Indispensable would float under the far bank for a moment before a fat, fighting three-quarter-pounder would rise and take it. I still remember the smell of those early days on Tweedside and if you put me there nowadays blindfold I'd know it in an instant, so firmly was it implanted in my impressionable brain.

My father had an uncle too who lived round the point from Tighnabruaich. He had a beautiful house overlooking the Kyles of Bute, a burn running through the garden into the sea and one of those beautiful old wooden motor launches with an inboard engine – *The Betty*. Trips to visit were wonderful for us youngsters; exploring the rhododendrons and woods, fishing in the burn for trout, and sea-fishing excursions in the evening. Uncle Jack would take us out for mackerel and haddock and we'd come back for a fry-up. The sound and taste of both, crisp and sizzling, had to be savoured to be believed. Jack would occasionally put out a net for sea trout at the burn mouth too and when the net was to be lifted there was always an air of huge expectancy. My father was usually enrolled for this physical chore and more often than not seaweed and jellyfish were the day's bounty.

'Pull harder, John,' Uncle Jack would cry, 'the net's all fankled.' Dad would pull harder and just now and again there would be the silvery shape of a sea trout. I couldn't believe how big and how beautiful they were and, like the old kelt, they fired a desire in me to fish for them in future.

A year or two later I had somehow acquired an old and very heavy nine-foot cane fly-rod, an ancient reel with an indeterminate line and no backing, 4 lb breaking-strain springy Luron nylon and about ten flies. I had yet to master the art of casting and was therefore more often than not stuck with fishing the worm. Not that it bothered me. I loved worming, and although it is frowned upon in some quarters, I still do to this day. The heart stopping rattle as a trout takes the bait still brings the same thrill. I'm not sure that the family was quite so thrilled, though. Every farm we passed, I would be commenting on the quality of their dung heaps and the possibility of stopping to ask the farmer if it might be possible to turn a bit of the sharn over to get at those red and yellow banded brandlings that the trout took so freely. Many a time when I got back in the car there was a lottery to see who would not sit beside me.

Those were heady days. We lived outside Edinburgh at Joppa, the posher end of Portobello (from the Spanish 'Beautiful Port' and known locally as the lungs of Edinburgh for its bracing sea air). Bracing and beautiful were perhaps not everyone's choice of adjective, but I loved it. I was down at the beach, the promenade and Joppa rocks at any opportunity. There was a crowd of folk who enjoyed fishing for flounders and mackerel from the prom or trying for crabs and eels among the seaweed on the rocks and digging for lugworm at low tide. But I still had a hankering

Joppa Beach flatties. Heriot's school trousers

to get to a riverside, use that rod and reel and try the flies for trout. And soon the chance came.

I was sent to 'do the messages' one Saturday morning, and, as I passed the terminus of the 15 bus, I noticed a slightly plump chap standing there in thigh waders and fishing-jacket and carrying a rod in his bag and a fishing-basket. Ever known for my powers of observation, I asked him if he was going fishing.

'Where the heck do you think I'm going?' he joshed. 'Do you think I always dress like this?'

I quickly realised he *was* going fishing and raked him with questions . . . Where? What to catch? How often do you go? How much does it cost? Where do you get a permit? How many fish do you catch? And can I come with you next time?

S'CUSE ME, ARE YOU GOING FISHING?

He patiently answered all of them and gave an affirmative to the last. Brilliant! Next Saturday I'd be off on the bus to Edinburgh, Peebles and the Lyne Water to fish properly for trout with my new friend. He was, and is, Mike Shepley, to this day my closest angling companion, director of the first series of *Hooked on Scotland* and a contributor to this book with his chapter on salmon fishing.

However, that first outing proved to be a mite frustrating. We got the bus to St Andrew Square; we got the bus to Peebles; we got the bus from Peebles to Glasgow and we got off beside the Five Mile Brig and started to fish our way downstream. The day was going mightily well. I caught a trout or two and was enjoying the feeling of being out fishing like a grown-up when Mike was suddenly not enjoying the feeling in his stomach. He was violently sick and we had to leave early. I was selfishly furious at having that first proper day's fishing curtailed. But it was the genesis of my fishing life and I will be eternally grateful to Mike for his part in it.

I started to read angling books and magazines. I bought *Angling Times*. This was a paper that mainly covered coarse fishing in England and I was enthralled with this new world. Regularly there were pictures of fish of 4, 5 and 6 lb with names that soon became familiar . . . roach, tench, bream, barbel, gudgeon, dace, rudd and perch. In fact, I was already acquainted with perch having, according to my old Lett's Boy Scout's Diary, 14 July 1959, taken 23 small perch from Duddingston Loch. But the size and variety of the fish in *Angling Times* amazed me. I joined their Kingfisher Guild, a club for young anglers, sent away for the list of rod-caught records, drooled over adverts for K. P. Morritt's of Cheam Intrepid reels and generally absorbed as much about any kind of fishing as I could.

The same year as the 23 perch, I visited Austria on a school trip. Innsbruck was beautiful, the Patscherkofel Mountain behind our modest hotel in Igls was magnificent, but what I remember most was a small lake which was stuffed with fish that would feed happily on bits of bread that I cast upon its water. I bought a couple of hooks and a spool of nylon and had a great time catching tiny roach and rudd without even using a rod. The breakfast rolls were secreted about my devious young person and off I'd go. I fished many times there and quite happily returned all the fish to the water. After all, wasn't that what the signs asked you to do? Not speaking much German, I had to guess at the meaning of '*Fischen Verboten*'.

A couple of years later on a family holiday (still in the Morris Minor!), we stopped near Pont St Esprit in the south of France for one of those fabulous holiday lunches. I must have been a right pain in the Arras as I was always asking if we could stop near a river or some piece of water, but more often than not my revered parents agreed. This particular day there was an elderly gent fishing with what I now know to be a roach pole. He was seated on a wicker basket at the tail of a pool and sort of dancing his bait across the surface – dapping, to all intents and purposes. In my tentative schoolboy French, I asked him what bait he was using and was told, '*Sauterelles*'. I may not have known '*Fischen Verboten*', but I did know a *sauterelle* from my elbow. He was fishing with live grasshoppers. We started to chat, me in rudimentary French and he in rude French, and, since I had a rod with me, he offered to help me to capture some bait. I'm sure the antics of this elderly Frenchman and young Scot tacking across the field by the river would have occasioned mirth, but it was a revelation to me the ability anglers have to communicate a common love of their sport across the language barrier. We caught a few grass-hoppers and with them a chub or two which M Clermont was delighted to take home to feed his family.

Meanwhile, back in Scotland horizons were broadening. Mike had caught a *huge* trout, 1 lb 6 oz from Portmore Loch, and I had my first ever 1 lb trout from the Tweed at Holylee. It actually weighed 1 lb 1 oz and I can still feel the thrill of the take over 30 years later. We had graduated from the Lyne to the Tweed and other waters and salmon had come into the frame.

We used to go to Perth Town Water on the first Saturday after opening day; as near as school would allow us to get to 15 January. Train to Waverley from Joppa (pre-Beeching), the 7.03 to Perth and then a walk through town with the waders on and all the gear to the Inch. We'd catch kelts, whitling and just now and again see the occasional springer being caught. All for five shillings a day.

We'd fish the Tyne at East Linton for trout and come home with roach and sea trout as well as the unexpected flounder. I caught sea trout at Yair on Tweed of 4½ lb (about the size of that old kelt that fired my enthusiasm so much!), and a brown trout of 4 lb 10 oz. This was a hen fish going back in condition, according to the lab at Faskally, and had four salmon parr and a water vole in the stomach when I cleaned it.

And I won a K. P. Morritt reel as a prize from the *Angling Times*. Bliss!

It was about this time that I started to venture further afield in Scotland. I was asked to play a part in a film being made by director Robert Irvine, some of which was to be

shot in Sutherland. Robert was a keen angler too and as
director he somehow managed to schedule filming so that
there was always a spot of spare time. One day we had
one of those wonderful walks in the hills at the back of
Inchnadamph. With a map, wellies and rod, plus nylon,
fly-box and a bite to eat in the fishing-bag, we followed the
map in a 13-mile round trip, fishing tiny lochans, burns
and lochs all along the way. Sometimes we'd come over a
crest and find several lochs in front of us and there was a
real delight in being able to argue as to who would fish
which! I can't remember exactly how many fish we caught,
but there were several good ones among the four-to-a-
pounders. Often we'd get three of these wee ones to splash
at the flies as soon as they hit the water but on other lochs
we would not even move a single trout, if, in fact, there
were any there in the first place. This kind of carefree
fishing is a scarce and precious commodity nowadays and I
sometimes wonder how long it will survive in tranquillity,
what with mountain bikes and mountain vehicles and the
rest making it all too easily accessible. Surely the walk is
part of the fun. Robert certainly enjoyed that part of the
world as he subsequently bought the Summer Isles Hotel
near Achiltibuie.

I visited Inchnadamph many times over the years and
had some wonderful fun. I went out one night on a
commercial boat from Lochinver to the Butt of Lewis. The
erudite skipper, Willie John, a great chess player, told me
that every Monday morning when he took the boat to sea in
rough weather he would be sea-sick for a short while, then
he'd be OK for the rest of the week. It was a fascinating
night and an eye opener for me to see how hard commercial
fishermen have to work for their living.

When we got back to the pier in the morning, Willie John
asked if I'd like to take a fish back for the hotel. He suggested a chicken halibut, a fish of about 10 lb which I
gratefully accepted. Now, as many of you who have fished
in the Highlands will know, hotels often display their

That reel-winning 4lb 10oz
Tweed brown trout

guest's catches on ashets in the foyer. So, for a giggle, I plonked the halibut on one, beside a small sea trout and a few brownies. As usual, the guests would wander from the bar, drinks in hand, to see who had caught what. One particularly plummy gent from well south of Hadrian's Wall asked me where I'd caught the big flounder. I told him I'd taken it on the dap on Loch Assynt and how it had come across the surface of the water like a manta ray and took in the Loch Ordie on the way down and how it gave one hell of a fight and barely fitted into the trout landing-net. The old gent tottered back to the bar for another large G and T muttering dark imprecations about youthful Scottish impudence – though I did hear later that he actually asked Willie Morrison if you could catch flounders on the fly!

Even further north lie those wonderful Orkney Isles. I first ventured there with Mike one November. We fished for ling out from Stromness off the Old Man of Hoy. The weather was coarse, the fishing was great, the people were wonderful and I fell in love with Orkney immediately. I also met a man who was to become another of my close friends. Ted Zawadzki owned Balfour Castle on Shapinsay and one of our first trips together was to Hoy one February to fish for sea trout on the coast. Mike, Ted, Johnny Riddle and myself lodged in digs at the old naval base at Lyness. In those days we just filled the car with petrol when we needed it and paid at the end of the trip. It was devilish cold that February, but bright, clear and calm. Rackwick looked stunning and we caught sea trout. Mike did well, quickly sussing out how to deal with the odd takes. The fish would take the sand-eel bait, dash off, drop it, come back and pick it up again and generally play about with it before taking it properly. However, we all got some fish and, despite the cold, the company was wonderful, the food was cheap, the drams were plentiful and friendships were forged that lasted for many years.

I had been asked to be a disc-jockey on Scotland's first commercial radio station at the beginning of 1966. Radio

Scotland came on air on 1 January and I had the privilege of uttering the first words: 'This is Radio Scotland on 242 metres in the medium wave', followed by our signature tune, *The Black Bear*. The life on the ocean radio waves was far from glamorous. The boat was old, cold and rolled. She was a converted lightship and when wind and opposing tide held her diagonally across the waves, it was not a comfortable place to be. The studio was in the stern and such was the amount of motion that in a big sea we would come down so far and so fast that the electric motors on the turntables would speed up and slow down the records. It played havoc with *'Donald, where's yer troosers?'*

But, of course, here was a ready-made fishing platform. We were anchored roughly halfway between Dunbar and the Isle of May in the outer Firth of Forth. I had taken some tackle with me, but the main problem was bait. Sometimes we were so short of food on the *Comet* that there was barely enough for the crew to eat – far less anything spare for me

The Comet *– where us pirates would mutiny for a bounty*

to use for the fishing. However, the fishing boats from
Dunbar would sometimes come alongside for a blether and
a cup of tea – yes, tea – and I chatted them up to see if they
had anything that might be useful. They had. Crayfish,
scampi or prawns. Call them what you will. They were but
a glint in the fish dealer's eye at this time and I was happily
given a couple of buckets of them every few days – not
much use as bait, but by jings they fairly livened up our
diet!

One day Tony Meehan, now a highly respected public
relations consultant, was on the air. There was a hatch
above the studio and I opened it gently and lowered a
fairly niffy fish caught the previous day. It dangled juicily
between Tony and the microphone and his comments were
hilarious. Juvenile perhaps, but we were allowed to do that
sort of childish thing. After all, we were pirates.

I spent nine months on Radio Scotland and I don't think I
caught more than a dozen fish the whole time. But I do
remember learning the intricacies of cribbage, sitting out
on deck at night in the pitch dark tracking the tiny white
pinpricks of satellites across the sky and occasionally looking at the lights on shore and wondering what all the lucky
folk there were up to. I thoroughly enjoyed my months as a
pirate, but was quite glad to fold the old skull and cross-
bones into a neat little parcel and become a land-based
lubber again.

Although I was no longer resident at sea, I still enjoyed
sea angling and, once I left the boat, actually I had more
opportunity to go sea fishing. These were exciting times
too. The famous Trio of Doug Dinnie, Bill Freshwater and
George Mann pioneered pirk fishing for cod on the Gan-
tocks, a wreck mark just off Dunoon. In their time they
probably caught more cod over 30 lb than any other group
in Europe and their activities were recorded for posterity
when Mike made a short film about them – *Run of the Wild
Fish*. My own successes were more mundane. I fished the
Lamlash Festival one year and won a dozen cans of beer. At

a February shore festival on the Clyde I was fifth out of 640 and won a landing-net. And on one Clyde outing from Fairlie with the BBC Club Angling Section in 1968 I had a haddock of 4½ lb. Nowadays that would be considered a miracle.

But I was graduating more towards freshwater angling. While Mike went on to represent Scotland and become European Champion in the sea-angling sphere, I found myself more involved in trout fishing with occasional forays for salmon. I was a member of the Heriot's FP Angling Club. While at that school, William B. Currie had been an English teacher. He was one of my angling heroes and I had read his many fishing books avidly from cover to cover time and time again. An angling club had been formed and it seemed logical to continue that enthusiasm into the FPs. We had regular outings and the most popular ones were to Loch Leven at Kinross. I was fascinated by the loch and over the years, like most anglers, was alternately frustrated and fulfilled by my visits.

I was first taken to Leven as a young lad by a friend of my father, and as there were no outboards on the boats, it depended on wind direction as to which end of the loch was the most favourable setting off point. There were two boatmen on the oars, but pick the wrong end on a breezy day and even these stalwarts would find it hard going to row back after a long drift. That first time, we went out from the sluice end. It was a bright day, I caught one fish, and I can still see it as the silvery shape came across the wave to take the fly. Once again I was captivated so much that I even defied parental control to get there.

A boat had been booked by Tommy Miller, a friend who had taken me under his wing, but on this occasion my mother had insisted that I was not to go fishing. Though it was to Loch Leven, permission was denied. But I would not be. I set the alarm for early, woke up two minutes before it went off, dressed in a trice, grabbed a few bits and pieces from the kitchen for my lunch and sneaked out of the house before the revered parents were awake. I ran up the road to Tommy's house and he gave me a bite of breakfast. I was shaking with excitement at the prospect of visiting 'the loch' and we got the train to Waverley and then the Perth connection. In those days quite a few anglers travelled by train and there was a jolly coterie discussing the prospects as we clanked across the Forth Bridge, lobbing the odd penny or halfpenny out of the window for good luck. The train chuffed into Kinross station and the fishers descended noisily on to the platform.

At the exit stood the stationmaster; big, ruddy – and ruddy well about to shatter my day. As we approached the gate, he announced in stentorian tones: 'Attention please attention. If there is a Paul Young going to fish Loch Leven, I have a message from your mother.'

Of course, I was mortified. I heard barely suppressed giggles as everybody turned to look for the elusive P. Young and knew exactly who he was!

'If there is a Paul Young going to fish Loch Leven, I have a message from your mother.'

I was on tenterhooks.

'Message reads . . . don't eat the pork pie, repeat, don't eat the pork pie.'

You can see what had happened.

Mother gets up, mother to kitchen to make breakfast, finds two-week old pork pie missing (no 'sell-by' dates then), panics and phones the station. Talk about embarrassed. But I consigned the pie to the loch and subsequently caught three trout. Speculate to accumulate, eh?

However, not all visits were so embarrassing. I had my share of good days and even finished up as club champion one year. It was a happy coincidence for me as the following year was the first of the *Daily Record*'s wonderful competition, 'The Champion of Champions'. This was open to any club champion but, due to the fact that there were 40 boats with three to a boat, only 120 anglers could be accommodated. Such was the interest in the angling world that over 300 entries far exceeded the places available and a ballot was held in which the Heriot Club was lucky enough to obtain a place. Anglers from all over Scotland took part in an excellent day. There was a marquee with coffee and snacks before the off, a half-bottle of whisky between the three anglers and a couple of cans of beer each.

I was in boat number seven and we finished up with most of the prizes. John Miller of Clackmannan Angling Club had the heaviest fish at 2 lb 13 oz. I had the best individual catch with four fish for 8 lb 6 oz and, together with Robert King of Forth and District Angling Club, we also had the heaviest boat catch with a six-fish total of 13 lb 10 oz. The Heriot Club won a welcome cash prize and I won some very welcome tackle. There was a buffet in the marquee later and the tales of lost fish and new-found friends were told again and again. One hundred and twenty anglers agreed it was a wonderful competition. I had to concur.

A few years later I was runner-up to the club champion, George 'Lucky' Dagger. As champion, George was entitled to fish in the National Championship, again at Loch Leven, but was not able to fish in the preliminary heat. So, as runner-up, I was honoured to fish in the annual champion-ship of the oldest National Angling Organisation in the world.

There were, once again, so many anglers eligible that two preliminaries were required to reduce the numbers and I fished the first one on 18 May 1974. Our boatman was the legendary Will Stark, a man who had fished the loch for many years and who knew it in all its moods. As the boats all sped off up the loch, he counselled that we should hang back, let the water settle and head for Castle Island where he had seen some good fish showing. It was grey, wet and calm and Will's reticence proved fruitful. We may have started later than others but my four fish of 2 lb 15 oz, 2 lb 10 oz, 2 lb 5 oz and 1 lb 15 oz were as fine a catch as you could ever wish for. An average of just under 2½ lb and enough to gain third place and a chance to fish in the final on 29 June.

That day I fished with Peter Keay and we had that wonderful character Bob Martin as our boatman. There were lots of fish moving and on the old favourites of a Dunkeld, Cinnamon and Gold, and a Hardy's Gold Butcher, once again I finished up with four fish, the last one coming late on and being crucial. It won me the coveted title of Scottish National Trout Fly Fishing Champion and a chance to fish for Scotland the following year.

It was a great thrill for me to represent my country at the sport I love and I fished internationals at Loch Leven in Scotland, Lake Trawsfynydd in Wales, where I was runner-up in the Scottish team, and Grafham in England, where Eric Campbell played a blinder, Scotland won and we all got a highly prized gold medal.

I'm aware that not everyone agrees that fishing should

A fine body of men – the Scottish fly fishing team

be a competitive sport and I can see their point of view, but I cannot deny that I am no less proud to have been a Scottish team member at fly-fishing than those who play football, rugby, badminton, darts or synchronised swimming.

Nor do I wish to give the impression that I only ever fished Loch Leven. For instance, I was acquainted with Loch Fitty before it became a commercial trout fishery. When the water was taken over by Game Fisheries Limited, I was kept abreast of what was happening by Iain MacKenzie, one of the directors of the company. Much work had to be done on this fertile water outside Dunfermline to remove coarse fish and provide facilities for trout anglers, and it is a great compliment to those involved over the years that it created, and then filled, a need for fishing that was inexpensive and accessible.

A 6 lb 4 oz fish from Loch Fitty. Only complaint . . . the bass is too small

Being basically a rainbow water, the dictates of fishing close seasons did not apply to those fish and the loch could happily open before the prescribed brown trout date of 15 March.

I have memories of some wild opening days at Fitty with rollers that would not shame the North Sea coming down the loch, but those who persevered were more often than not rewarded with some good fish. The opposite often met you there too; flat calm summer evenings with fish showing everywhere but proving almost impossible to catch. Many a time I was driven demented as the shoals of fish, for so it seemed, nosed upwind and studiously ignored every fly, nymph or lure that was gently laid in their path. Mind you, on those nights there was often a real fisher who could work out what the fish were on and he or she would come in with a handsome catch. As with those early chilly days, it was, and still is, a pleasure to come into the well-stocked fishing lodge for tea or coffee and a blether about where you were going wrong. Iain's son Gerald now manages the Loch and it is good to see a continuity of enthusiasm, whereby the angler's wants and needs are

catered for and Gerald's mother Florence still makes a
mean bacon roll.

One of my first contacts with the 'new face' of trout
angling occurred at Linlithgow Loch where I watched an
angler fishing from an anchored boat. He was casting an
extremely long line, letting it sink for what seemed an
inordinate time and stripping it back far faster than anyone
I had seen before. He took quite a few trout that day too,
the best of which weighed a shade over 4 lb. He was also
fishing a very odd-looking fly. It was tied solely with white
wool and he told me it was called a Baby Doll and worked
well for rainbows on English reservoirs. I managed to
obtain some, along with a fast sinking line, and, again at
Linlithgow, had five fish up to 3¼ lb. They were beautiful
trout too, a touch of olive green on the back contrasting
with the vivid white of the belly. I enjoyed many days on
Linlithgow.

As I have done on the Lake of Menteith, arguably the
most beautiful of the managed fisheries in lowland Scotland. Like Fitty, I have memories of the lake before it was
stocked with rainbows. I had fished for Menteith pike,
been stranded on Inchmahone Island in a gale and seen
one or two of the magnificent brownies taken by pike
fishers on the troll. One fish of about 3 lb seemed to me to
embody the perfect trout in shape and colour; small head,
wide Teddy Boy shoulders and colour straight from an
artist's palette.

Since the lake was stocked with rainbows, I have fished
there many times with many different companions and
none has failed to be impressed by the setting. I've never
had any of the really big fish that are there, but I've seldom
been disappointed in my day, fishless or fortunate. One
day in particular I watched an osprey quarter the water not
30 yards from the boat before folding its wings and falling
in a graceful parabola on an unsuspecting rainbow. The
bird climbed about ten feet and I could see the water
droplets glint in the sun as the trout writhed in the osprey's

talons. About 20 feet up the bird ruffled its feathers and another shower sparkled in the light. Gracefully and surprisingly slowly, the osprey gained height and leisurely disappeared into the trees with the fish supper for its chicks. I can't remember if I had fish for my own chickens that day, but somehow it didn't seem to matter.

In 1977 a chance came up for a most exciting trip. Mike was by now established as a film-maker and we had previously made an angling film in Ireland. *Return to Paradise* was a visual interpretation of an English angler's happy obsession with Irish trout fishing. We filmed in County Clare on Lake Inchiquin among others and, as with every trip to Ireland, you come away richer for the experience and vowing to return. This time, though, we were bound for further afield. We were off to Greenland on behalf of the Danish Tourist Board to show the quality of the fishing there, with special reference to the migratory Arctic char.

Greenland was magnificent. We had called at Keflavik in Iceland on the way from Copenhagen and, as we came

The body beautiful(?) Fishing for Arctic char among the icebergs

towards the Greenland coast, the sea changed from deep blue to aquamarine to palest blue dotted with icebergs. The plane banked sharply over the fjord and dropped quickly on to the runway of the old US Air Force base of Bluie West One at Narsarsuaq, sometimes spelled Narssarssuaq!

It was mid-August and the mornings were misty but mild. Around noon the mist would lift and we generally had sun for the rest of the day. The rivers we fished were of two kinds. There was the milky water of the Qingua that came from melting ice, glaciers and the like and there was the crystal clear spring water of Ingeborg's pool. We fished both and caught fish in both. Yellow was a popular colour of fly and the Arctic char fought like demons. They were not large fish, up to a couple of pounds plus perhaps, but even sea trout would be hard put to match their power. Just when you thought they were coming to the net, they'd be off again, game to the last. We kept a few and cooked them in tinfoil for lunch. Our Greenlandic guide, Friedrik, looked askance as we left the heads having eaten the flesh. To him the heads were the best part and the eagerness with which he devoured them was a joy to see.

We went sea fishing too and it was awesome as we threaded our way between icebergs that dwarfed our boat. Near Qoroq Fjord we could hear the bergs calving from the glacier with a crack and groan that carried for miles. And sometimes a berg of a hue so blue that it looked as if it was lit from within by an ultra violet light would gently heel over. The sea, being that bit warmer, would melt the sub-surface ice until it became top heavy. So-o-o slowly, thousands of tons of frozen water would heel over and send a series of oily waves across the calm sea.

We saw two parent and two young white-tailed sea eagles fly slowly past us and, as we followed them up the valley, we came to a peak above which the thermals allowed the eagles and a dozen or so ravens to wheel and mingle in the up-draught. They looked like black snowflakes on a breeze.

One morning we were dropped off to fish a lake and the short river, the Ilua, linking it to the fjord. We were due to be picked up around 5 p.m. but by about 6.30 we knew something was wrong. Come 8.00, a launch arrived and told us that our boat was out of commission with an electrical fault. The prospect of a night in the open in Greenland filled none of us with joy. The sky was inky black pricked white by millions of stars. There was no habitation near and next stop down the fjord was Baffin Land. We were eventually picked up by a replacement boat close to midnight, though. As we moved through the water, the skipper scanned the surface in front with a searchlight, looking for ice in our path. I lay at the bow, peering into the dark, with the beam piercing the blackness ahead and picking out the white shapes to be avoided. When we got back to the Arctic Hotel, we were all given a huge dram to celebrate our safe return – I can tell you, few have ever tasted so sweet.

Greenland was a real adventure from start to finish; a beautiful country with great traditions and, if pressed to describe the area in the south-west where we had been filming, I'd be tempted to say it was like Glencoe . . . with icebergs.

Dubai is not. That was the next exotic location that I visited with Mike. He was establishing a reputation in the Middle East and had been commissioned to make a short film extolling the virtues of Dubai as a business centre. He needed a 'businessman' to move through all the Emirate has to offer, and I got the job.

Dubai is a fascinating blend of old and new. Down at the Creek you could see motorised dhows piled high with everything from spices and fruit to refrigerators and air-conditioning systems bound for Karachi. The crews would be on deck cooking their meals and the smells were heady and intoxicating. The colours were rich and varied and there were also the *abbras*, the water taxis, plying back and forth laden with people from many different races.

For me, it was my first taste of the Arab world and I loved it.

We were filming one evening at Jumeirah Beach. It was close to sunset and Mike wanted some silhouette shots of an angler on the beach casting towards the sun setting on the horizon. We had some tackle and a bit of frozen barracuda as bait, which I managed to lob a few yards into the surf where we had enjoyed an invigorating dip earlier in the day. I had no thought of catching anything on this fairly crude set-up, and was happily acting away for the camera when the top of the rod suddenly dipped and I was into a fish. I tightened and it shot off parallel to the beach. It was strong, but after a few minutes I managed to bring it close to the water's edge. I still couldn't see what it was, so Mike eventually waded in and brought out a guitar fish – halfway between a shark and a skate . . . flat underneath with shark-like upper parts. It had a spiked tail and, while I was thrilled to catch such an unusual specimen (for me), I was a bit worried to think that I'd earlier been sharing the water with this spiky character.

We also spent a day trying for sailfish. We left harbour in the cool of early morning and scanned the smooth waters of the Gulf for signs of sea birds working on shoals of baitfish, knowing that our prey wouldn't be far away. It was a new experience for me to be game fishing at sea, and the outriggers, fighting chair and big game rods and reels lent to the atmosphere. We came across sea birds wheeling and screaming and could see fish showing on the surface. Out went the baits. We were trolling on the surface with small silver fish called balao; two on the outriggers and two from the back of the boat. The skipper took us in broad circles round the still erupting baitfish and it wasn't long before the thrilling sight of that tell-tale dorsal of a sailfish appeared briefly behind one of them. I was handed the rod, the line was taken from the outrigger and I was told to tease the fish by lifting and lowering the rod – giving and taking the bait from the fish's reach. Again the sail showed and next thing the bait was taken with a lunge and the reel screamed as the fish set off fast.

I was with folk who had landed many sailfish and, being the only 'virgin', I took their advice readily. I waited until I was told and, at the right moment, flicked the reel into gear, watched the line lift and struck hard. The bait came out of the water and, there being no resistance, I tottered backwards, clattered my head on the wheelhouse and fell, half-stunned, to the deck.

Moments like these are when true friends show their worth. I obviously had few at that time as everyone roared with laughter and I was thrown a can of cold beer with which either to drown my sorrows or bathe my aching napper. I think we had runs from five or six fish that day and not one was hooked – though I did have the consola-

A mean-looking hunting machine . . . with barracuda

tion of catching my first-ever barracuda. Of course, my Dubai visit was far too short to explore more than a fraction of the fishing potential and I can't wait to get back for an in-depth fishing trip.

Another excursion that was way too short was one to California. I'd been jammy enough to be cast as First Officer Murdoch in *SOS Titanic*, a three-hour television movie being made about that great ship's maiden voyage. We had filmed at Shepperton studios in England, but the director required some exterior shots of the ship so we found ourselves living and working on the *Queen Mary* at Long Beach, where the old ship would be used as the *Titanic*'s double.

Murdoch was the officer on watch when the ship hit the iceberg, so I was involved in quite a bit of filming, most of which was done on the bridge. It felt strange to be up there amidst all the magnificent brass and wood and to think she was built not far from where I now live. I'd had to travel over 5,000 miles for my first sight of her, and I felt intensely proud of all the Scotsmen and women who had crafted her so lovingly.

Filming was mainly at night, so we had several days off and I hired a car and drove up Pacific Coast Highway 1 to Santa Monica to visit friends. I also managed to squeeze in a fishing trip early one morning on the *Indiana* out from Santa Monica pier. It was very misty and the pier was quickly out of sight. In fact, apart from the accents of the other anglers, we might have been anywhere . . . out from Largs on a misty Scottish morning perhaps.

Though in Largs you'd be unlikely to catch a brown pelican. One of the anglers beside me was trotting his live anchovy bait downtide (also not often seen at Largs!) when out of the mist like a ton of bricks the pelican crashed into the water in front of us and took his bait. There was pandemonium as it splashed on the surface and the skipper got hold of the line and slowly drew the bird to the boat. The pelican glared malevolently at him and tried to spear

A cast on board Queen Mary, *Long Beach, California*

him with its long pouched beak. Obviously well used to dealing with dischuffed pelicans, the skipper flipped the bird under his arm, caught the beak in his gloved hand, nicked the hook out and threw the bird skywards all in one deft movement. It was so surprised, it collapsed in a pile of huffy feathers, threw us all a dirty look and rather untidily, pride sorely dented, took off into the morning mist.

The fishing was interesting too with hard-fighting bonito as well as Pacific mackerel, barracuda, dogfish and sand-bass. I was returning all my fish when one of the other anglers asked if I'd give him any of the sand-bass I caught as they were the only fish his kids would eat. I happily gave him the three or four I took later and for each one was rewarded with a can of cold beer. Lovely folks, Californians.

Mind you, despite all this gallivanting, Scotland was, and still is, the focal point of my fishing.

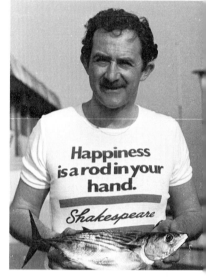

Sure is!

Salmon had come more into the frame and, though I'd had one or two fish here and there, it was all a bit chuck and chance it, especially with the fly, until, that is, Ted Zawadzki invited me to share a rod with him on the River Conon one July. I was taken down to the river on arrival and the sight of salmon and grilse heading and tailing in profusion got me palpitating. I was shaking so much that I could barely tie on my fly. Ted took me down to the Boat Pool, a long, deep pool lined by trees on both banks and more easily fished from the water. We were both seated on a plank across the stern and Johnnie MacDonald the ghillie let us down the pool on an anchored rope. Ted kindly gave me the rod and, as instructed, I tried to drop the tiny Stoat's Tail under the trees and let it swing out into the centre of the current. After about three casts I saw a tail show just behind the fly and felt the line pull fairly firmly.

Now, I'd done a fair amount of trout fly fishing but little for salmon, so, of course, I struck as soon as I felt the take. The fish came in a flurry to the surface, rolled twice and was away. Ted was horrified.

'Call yourself an angler?' he roared. 'Bluddy troot fishers,' he yelled in his wonderful half-Polish half-Scottish English. It was delicately explained that one should give the fish time to take the fly and *then* gently tighten. I was given a second chance. Same again. Fish took, I struck, fish boiled, fish off, tongue lashing from Ted. Third time, a repeat of the first two and by now Ted and Johnnie were roaring with laughter at my ineptitude.

It was at this moment that Ted offered me a bit of advice that I always remember when I'm salmon fly-fishing. He said that he would tie a length of strong nylon to one particularly vulnerable part of my anatomy, take the nylon a couple of times round the rod and tie it to the matching precious orb so that, the next time I struck a salmon take on the fly, I'd pull both orbs from their natural setting – and I would only do it once. The fact that I might never subsequently father children and only be fit for employment as a choirboy or a bouncer (unfortunate word perhaps) at a harem, helped to imprint Ted's device indelibly in my brain. It works a treat, though. To this day before I start fishing with the fly, I think of Ted's device and over the years have seldom been too quick on a take – and any time I have, I've always felt that tweak of apprehension in my gut . . . or thereabouts.

I learned a lot on those Conon summers. The river is the last part of a hydro-electric scheme that spreads far to the west, and below the Torr Achilty dam there is always a basic compensation flow of water. When the turbines are generating, the river-level can rise by up to about four feet depending on the power being generated so that you can be fishing what amounts to several different rivers in the course of a day. Fish obviously move to more convenient lies as the water-level rises and falls and it was great exercise of the fishing brain to read the river in all its variety.

Ted and I shared a rod for many years, firstly with a wonderful woman, Mrs 'Towser' Lowe. On one memorable day we had 18 fish to the two rods . . . all summer salmon and grilse and all on very small flies. Towser had five, Ted six and I had seven, my best-ever daily total. As we relaxed in the evening in the primitive comfort of the old fishing caravan, Johnnie said what a pity it was that we hadn't got just one more as we'd have created a new record daily catch. Of course, we tacked back to the river in the dusk to try and happily, failed miserably.

A few years later, Ted and I joined up with Denis Lennox. Denis was a big man in many ways. Hugely generous, greatly humorous and a man who generated fun wherever he went. His Billy Connolly impressions had to be heard to be believed. The caravan would shudder in the evenings as Johnnie, with tears of laughter running down his face, Ted and I would watch Denis almost burst as the guffaws convulsed him. We caught fish too. In one drought year we took it in turns to have three casts on the only bit of water where fish could be covered. The Pulpit was a difficult long cast to the other side of a fast stream from a high rock. You had to mend about three times to get the four or five seconds when the fly would fish where the salmon were lying on the far side of the current before being whipped into the main stream where the fish weren't lying. And three casts covered it. So, turn about it was and in between, back to the caravan for another revivifying dram.

We finished the week with over 20 fish and as many empty bottles. Other years of good water, we worked harder for sometimes fewer and sometimes more. But always there was the laughter. Ted lived in his Shapinsay castle, Denis on his Shropshire estate and me in a tenement in Maryhill but we were united by the joy of fishing.

With Ted's device firmly in mind, I have since fished some fine salmon water in Scotland. I've had to save hard on many occasions, but it has often been worth it.

The famous Junction Pool, where Teviot meets Tweed at Kelso, was kind to me on a couple of occasions. Under the arches of the main road bridge, a bit of water not always fished, I took the only salmon of the day on fly as others persevered with their spinners. And below, at Hempseedford, I thought I was finished with the pool, made one last cast, turned and started to wade back to shore with the rod over my shoulder. Two steps and the reel screamed as a fish took the fast moving fly. Eleven-and-a-half pounds of silvery Tweed springer was my some-what undeserved reward.

We were fishing Lower Norham one day in early autumn. The river was low and there was a good head of fish waiting for water, but they were not in taking mood. I was sitting with Ian Calcott having lunch when an angler from the beat above weaved his way down the bank towards us. He'd obviously had a fair amount of liquid for his lunch and probably for his breakfast and elevenses too! But he was in good spirits and, when we told him that we'd caught nothing so far, he suggested an old local remedy. In a broad Leeds accent, he advised us to 'stone t'bloody pool' and proceeded to lob several large boulders into the neck where fish had been showing all morning.

'That'll stir t'boogers oop,' he cried, and disappeared back to his own beat. Ian and I were somewhat perplexed to take five fish between us from that same spot in the afternoon. Our visitor had been a little stoned, the pool had been well stoned and we caught several stone of salmon. Funny old game.

Mike and I were fishing the Nith late one year. We'd been with White Horse Whisky the day before for their popular Clyde Shore Festival and they had several Japanese guests. These anglers had won competitions at home, the prize being a trip to Scotland to fish the White Horse, followed by a day salmon fishing. They had acquitted themselves well in the Shore Festival, but were somewhat fazed on arriving at the beat on the Nith. Where was everybody? The lack of fellow anglers amazed them and they found it hard to believe all that water was just for them. A salmon was caught in the morning and at lunch-time they went to work. A sharp knife removed a portion of flesh which was then finely sliced. Various condiments appeared as if by magic and we were all treated to Japanese-style raw salmon accompanied by Scottish-style mature whisky. On a cold, misty November riverbank, the two cultures came together magnificently and both elements of the meal tasted superb.

On that wonderful salmon river, the Aberdeenshire Dee, I was fortunate enough to fish on Her Majesty the Queen Mother's beat at Birkhall. It is lovely water and the first time I fished there I had a 10-pounder within a few minutes of starting. Easy-peasy, thought I, and, of course was gloriously wrong. Over several visits, that was the only salmon I ever caught, though I did have one good night with half-a-dozen sea trout up to 3½ lb. Difficult water to wade by day, in the dark it was a nightmare. I hear it is a favourite bit of water of His Royal Highness, the Prince of Wales, but if he can wade it easily, he is a better, or braver man than I.

But the Dee brought me pounds of a different kind on another occasion. There is a lovely pool on Birkhall called Polveir and just above it is a fastish run and holding water known as Little Polveir. Now, I am not really a betting man – the Derby and the Grand National are my limit – but a few years ago I noticed that there was a horse running in the National called Little Polveir. Worth a flutter, I thought, and put a few quid on the nose. It won handsomely, thereby furnishing me with the wherewithal to purchase a few more blank Dee days.

My favourite salmon river of all is the Helmsdale. Some-times called the 'Queen of Rivers', it certainly reigns supreme in my book. It has every type of water that a salmon fly-fisher could wish for – glides, streams, moor-land flats that you have to read, falls, rickles and popply runs – there is hardly a bit of that river where you don't think you'll get a fish, even for a fairly inexpert caster like

me. It is big enough to challenge and, in places, small enough to be difficult.

Mike and I started our Helmsdale fishing with a week in February and it could be fairly chilly. Salmon fishing at this time of year is laughingly known as 'Spring fishing'. More than once we had to break the ice to fish and we also had the odd game of rudimentary curling on the frozen flats. We were lucky enough to move a week or two later and now fish in the middle of March. It can still be cold, but we generally manage to have an ice-free week. Our ghillie, Johnnie Sutherland, known as Johnnie Hardy because he is, is a wonderful character and companion. Singer, raconteur, cabaret artiste and jokester . . . these are all things he'd like to be! But there is seldom a dull moment on the river bank when Johnny is about and he knows the river in all its moods. I've had a few fish over the years and I know I wouldn't have had half of them without Johnny's patient and helpful prompting. A great character and friend and there is always the bonus of a plate of his wife Betty's wonderful soup to heat you up after a nippy day on the river.

As well as being generally frost-free, March has another bonus in the quality of the fish. Sea-liced, firm-fleshed hard-fighting springers are the absolute nonpareil. One day of horizontal sleet, we cowered in the hut for longer than usual at lunchtime, had an extra dram to warm us up and I bored everyone rigid with a rendering of *Tam o' Shanter*. As if taking pity on the others, the weather improved and out we went. Within minutes of starting, both Mike and I hooked fish which fought well before coming to the net. When they were laid out on the step of the hut, they were within an inch of each other in length – but mine was a deep, chunky fish and Mike's longer, slimmer and more typically Helmsdale. An American footballer alongside a cricketer. Mike's weighed just over 9 lb and mine was almost 13½ . . . nearly 50 per cent heavier.

March is also the time when the country begins to wake

Brothers Johnnie and George Sutherland, fine Helmsdale ghillies both up after winter. Many a day you'll see salmon leaping, deer on the skyline and the eagle quartering its territory high in the hills. Weasels jink along the riverbank, rabbits dive for cover and the plovers return to the fields. The days are lengthening, there is a touch of warmth in the sun and sometimes a fish on the bank at the end of the day. Perfection.

Rivers such as the Tay, North Esk, South Esk, Stinchar and Eachaig have all been kind to me at times and, as ever, the company is as important as the fishing. I love being with and listening to people with the angling bug. Andy Pelc talking of his beloved South Esk sea trout; Dougie Stewart, the Tay boatman, talking enthusiastically in colourful terms of how a fish was landed; or being with James Hay as we tweak each other's brains for the derivation of some word or phrase on our way to that lovely little river, the Fyne. For me, fishing is more than just the sum of its parts. It is often possible to have a wonderful day without even seeing a fish. And there can be times when catching fish after fish may reduce the pleasure of the day. Without some sort of challenge to overcome, success is not so sweet.

I know I've been lucky over the years whether catching grayling on Teviot, sea trout on the Endrick or perch in Duddingston Loch. And even luckier recently to have been asked to present *Hooked on Scotland*. To go round this wonderful country of ours trying to catch fish and chatting to interesting people is a joy. But at home, I can't let everybody know what a privilege and pleasure it is. When the kids ask me, 'What did you do today, Daddy?', I tell them I was out filming people fishing and that it is cold and lonely work – but somebody's got to do it!

HELLO SALAR

Michael Shepley

'Or like the snow falls in the river
A moment white then melts forever'

'Season of mists and mellow fruitfulness . . .'

For generations, poets have praised and composers com-
plimented the seasons of the year. W. Earl Hodgson, a
salmon and trout man of some renown, writing at the
beginning of this century, declared the cycle of spring,
summer, autumn and winter 'very fine indeed'. He recounts
the tale of a poet who wrote an ode to the four seasons,
proclaiming each to be the best of all the year. A perplexed
observer remarked that surely each of the seasons couldn't
be the best, and in his praise of each to the detriment of the
others, had the poet not denounced them all?

'How do I reconcile the odes? I don't do it at all!' replied
the poet. 'I, with the seasons, am like that great man, Lord
L—— with the ladies. He always said he never was in love
but once, and that was with the last one!' I am sure Robert
Burns would have agreed.

To place salmon and fishing for them into four seasons is
logical, as well as chronological, and like Earl Hodgson, I
too, confess to finding it hard to choose a favourite time.

A great pal of mine, Ian Bain, defined the dedicated
salmon angler as: '. . . a true devotee to the sport, one who
will defy physical and sometimes financial hardship in the
pursuit of a passion, where every cast holds the essence
of anticipation.'

I freely admit to being one of the great Band of Hope who, albeit foolishly, always think that the next cast is going to produce a salmon.

The Atlantic salmon, *Salmo salar*, is undoubtedly one of the great wonders of the natural world. Its migratory instincts take it from the streams of its birth across the seas to feed off Greenland. And then, one year or several more later, it returns to Iceland, the British Isles, Mainland Europe, Canada or North America . . . to its native river, to spawn and continue the cycle of life and death.

Unlike the various species of Pacific salmon, not all Atlantic salmon die after spawning, although many do. Neither do they all spawn in the headwaters of rivers, a simplification and inaccuracy perpetuated by many angling books. Large numbers of salmon spawn in the middle and lower reaches wherever there is suitable gravel – even just above the tide. Early run salmon, the 'springers', will head for the hills, travelling miles and living off the reserves of their own oil-rich flesh. The grilse of the summer months will not run so far upstream, and many of the autumn arrivals will stay in the lower reaches.

There is a complicated, but well-defined order of things *salmonoid* in our Scottish rivers, beginning with the youngsters, alevins and parr, which eventually migrate to saltwater as silvery smolts and return as adult salmon. There is also that wonderful sporting fish, the sea trout, sadly absent from many of its past haunts, and there are the brown trout and grayling which compete with the immature salmon for food. Sometimes other coarse fish are present too, such as roach, dace and perch.

Fish farming may have been a much-welcomed alternative to unemployment in the Highlands and Islands, but it has also brought us environmental chaos; not just of the visual kind, but for the wild fish also. Farmed salmon and saltwater-reared rainbow trout escape in their thousands each year. And nobody yet knows the long-term effects. The scientists will quite rightly be slow to point a fishy finger until they are satisfied that their research is as complete as technically possible. But we do now know that farm salmon spawn with wild fish; and sea-run rainbow escapees which enter our salmon rivers no doubt play havoc on the spawning redds. In North America the wild, sea-run rainbows, known as steelheads, play their part in regulating the overwhelming spawning of the many Pacific salmon species. Here, they could well spell disaster for the future of the Atlantic salmon.

But this is not a book of conjecture or criticism, but a celebration of things piscatorial. And of Scotland's fishes, *Salmo salar*, the leaper, is the greatest of them all.

HEAD AND SHOULDERS – EARLY SPRING

Just after the mists of Hogmanay have cleared a week or ten days or so, the first small groups of that sub-species, *Piscator salmo springus*, break hibernation and emerge from both stupor and torpor. In the early part of the season, when fulfilment often falls far short of the mark and passions pall with the numbness of icy water and bitterness of the wind, I often think that salmon fishers (and I am a dedicated member of that club) are just a little bit mad. Many observers and the uninitiated would unhesitatingly certify each and every one of us.

On 15 January each year (unless that date falls on the Sabbath) the salmon season on Perthshire's mighty River Tay opens with all the pomp and circumstance befitting such a monarch as the King of Scotland's fishes. Everyone is an expert, especially once the amber liquid starts to flow. Questions and answers shoot across the big pools as fast as the spoons, plugs and spinners meant to attract the salmon.

'Do ye ken more?'

'Naw, I said d'ye ken Kenmore?'

The general idea is that the first boat of the season is

'blessed' by a bottle of whisky. Nowadays, to save environmentally unfriendly broken glass flying in every direction, a silver quaich is used to deposit the whisky over the bows and dispatch the boat on its way. I also suspect that the aforementioned quaich holds somewhat less than the usual 75 cl!

As the morning hiccups towards midday, one or two fish are inevitably hooked . . . some even landed. Most are kelts, the spawned salmon on their return journey back down the river to the open sea.

The word 'kelt' to layman and international visitor obviously poses a problem. One puzzled American visitor, observing an angler hooking then returning two salmon to the river, was heard to query: 'The fish wore kilts?'

'No sir,' the ghillie replied with well-defined understanding, '. . . the fish *were kelts*!'

It seems hardly an hour since some of the boats left the small pier below the hotel; indeed, it is barely an hour. But then it's lunchtime, and opening day at Kenmore is as much about celebrating the fact, as actually going fishing.

'Hey . . . is that bottle named after Miss Georgina? . . . Whit wus the weight . . . 64 pund? Jeees, that's only 53 pun heavier than ma best fush!'

'It's amazing how the air hits you when you get out of the boat!' laughs one well-seasoned exponent of the angle . . . from the middle of a gorse bush.

His pal stands in the stern of the boat, looking at his lure box while mis-quoting Shakespeare: 'Toby or not Toby . . . that is the question!'

I remember one opening day at Kenmore. The river was very high and little if anything had been taken from the big pool below the bridge. Loch Tay was also very high, and the press of water coming through the arches made it very difficult to push a boat into the loch, even with the outboard going full throttle.

Paul Young and I had been watching half a dozen big salmon holding station on the edge of the current. We could see one particular fish clearly because it had a spot of disease on its head. A salmon of perhaps 15 or 16 lb, he was lying hard to the middle stanchion of the bridge, using the back pressure off the front edge of the pillar to ease his efforts.

'Those fish lying above the bridge *never*, *ever* take, you know,' ventured an onlooker. 'There's no point even bothering to fish for them.' By the loud manner, and even louder Tweed jacket, breeks and matching nose, I took the gentleman to be a visitor rather than a local.

'Then . . . how do you know if they ever take or not?' I responded, not wishing to sound provocative, but obviously failing miserably.

I hoped our sage would be in the bar later that evening when we arrived back at the hotel with a handsome 17-pounder, one of the small cluster of salmon lying close to the middle stanchion of the bridge. Had Paul not been at the helm, it would have been his silver sprat and not mine which had proved the fatal attraction.

In Perthshire, 15 January is to the salmon fisher what 12 August is to the glorious 12-bore enthusiast. But further north, the opening of the salmon season precedes the Tay by several days. And if not greeted with quite the same display of well-publicised pastiche, the enthusiasm and expertise are perhaps even greater. This is fly fishing country. And the names of the rivers are famous far beyond the boundaries of Scotland: Helmsdale, Naver, Thurso and Brora.

The flies that lure the early-season springers are a celebration of famous fishers and favourite casts – Willie Gunn, Megan, Jock Scott, Yellow Torrish, Garry Dog, Green Highlander . . . If someone mentions 'the hair of the dog', it's as likely to refer to tying flies as an early dram for medicinal purposes!

The wonderful built-wing flies which were still in vogue in my youth have given way to simplified, but highly effective, hair-wing varieties: bucktail, squirrel and even collie dog hair. My Pariah dog, Halley, all the way from the Middle East, has a superb, shiny coat of densest black and creamy white, varying in length and ideally suited to everything from a three-inch Waddington to a number 12 long-shanked double. He doesn't know it, but he ties a splendid fly – and they catch salmon too!

It's supposed to be *bad luck* to wish somebody good luck or 'tight lines!' You'll hear the phrase, 'Wet nets and leaky boots!' far more, although if you have ever suffered from leaky boots yourself, you wouldn't wish them on anybody, even your worst adversary. Of course, you need not have leaky boots to get wet. Falling in will do nicely! And I doubt if there are many regular anglers who haven't done it once or twice in their career.

On wading for salmon, William Scrope, that great early piscator and author from the Borders, observed:

> Pull down your stockings and examine your legs. Should they be black, or even purple, get on dry land, but if they are only rubicund, you may continue to enjoy the water.

Scrope was no doubt denied the comfort of chest waders when fishing for his salmon, but they don't always guarantee freedom from either the cold or the damp. I've often seen my arrival at the waterside coincide with the realisation that all was not well – the leak I'd forgotten to patch, or the misjudgment of the last barbed-wire fence before the river bank, resulting in a new tear *below* the water-line. And of course, as we all remember from our school science days, the water level *inside* the waders doesn't stay level with the leak zone, but matches the depth outside the waders. The deeper you go, the wetter you get!

For me, the epitome of early-season salmon fishing is the long drive up to Sutherland and Caithness in January, February and March, to cast a line over those wonderful peat-coloured pools and streams. Just occasionally there is a strong pull and the flash of silver as a fresh-run salmon takes the fly. There are no better fish than these springers.

It was mid-February, and we were making our way up the Strath . . . slowly. Outside the car we could just about see either side of the road, but not ahead. Sheep appeared as grubby smudges on a whiter-than-white landscape . . . then just as suddenly disappeared, enveloped in the swirls of snow.

I pulled the car gently over into what I hoped was the usual layby opposite the railway viaduct on Beat 1. The heavy snow blanketed everything save the sound of the unseen river and a solitary curlew. It was eerie.

As my eyes grow accustomed to the brightness of the light, I can make out the River Helmsdale where it cuts a deep, dark gash across the whiteness. The snow starts again, and although I'm only a few feet away from the car, I

Parking problems

can hardly see Johnny Hardy assembling the second rod for my guest, Steve Morris from Hale, Cheshire.

Within minutes of setting up the rod and casting into a stream reasonably clear of ice, the line is already freezing to the rod-rings and the big Waddington Willie Gunn looks for all the world like a miniature Christmas tree. Steve's still in the back of the car.

'You're not seriously fishing in that?' he asks with incredulity as the snow flakes increase in size and intensity.

'Steve, come on out, the weather's fine; everyone knows that the bigger the flakes, the milder the air temperature.' He looks seriously worried. Mind you it's his first time so far north at this time of year. I try to tell him he'll get used to it . . . might even enjoy the experience, but there's no further movement.

Steve's arrival in Helmsdale had, in fact, caused quite a stir. His swarthy good looks, fine gold-rimmed glasses and close-cropped beard complemented the Arab head-dress which added a note of bright colour to his Barboured ensemble. The fact that he had offered to pay for the groceries with a mixed basket of Pan-Arabian currency from Dirhams to Riyals was, I felt, a masterly stroke which sent a buzz running up the Strath faster than a summer grilse. It took a little convincing later – and a few good drams – to reassure some of the ghillies that they would not have a new owner on the river.

In January and February I have seen the river frozen from bank to bank following overnight frost, and, on one auspicious occasion, passed a pleasant couple of hours on Baddy Wood with Paul Young and our ghillie Johnny, not fishing, but curling! A little further upstream we dis-covered where a dog otter had made a catch and dragged the salmon out of the water over a shelf of marginal ice on to the bank. All that was left were a few scales and the imprints of his foot pads.

During times of hard frost, it is actually possible to break the ice into large rafts and float them off downstream. After several hours' hard work, which can keep you warm in the process, the pools can be fished and, if you're lucky, can reward you with a fresh-run springer, a salmon which will have run upstream under the ice for several miles.

Angling author Bill Currie, a regular early-season fisher on the Helmsdale has had his share of such fish after breaking up the ice, but it can be hard and long work. Once he had two salmon for a whole week's effort . . . an 8-pounder and another of 28 lb!

Spring fish on the Helmsdale are amongst the finest and largest of the season. I've seen a 27-pounder and a sea-liced 20-pounder, both from the Manse Pool on Beat 6, a great early-season big-fish lie.

After breaking up, early-season fishing can also mean 'backing up', a method on slower water whereby the angler starts at the tail of the pool, rather than at the head stream which is the norm. Casting across and downstream, the angler walks slowly and carefully (watch the gorse bushes and rabbit holes!) upstream, hand-lining as he goes. This has the effect of increasing the speed at which the fly fishes over the lies, and also presents the fly suddenly to the fish which is facing upstream rather than from above, where the fish has more opportunity of seeing the fly approach down the pool. This often results in an induced take of some ferocity. Salmon seldom miss the target. It's an exciting way of fishing!

As with all early rivers, these Highland streams generally have a large number of kelts dropping back seawards after spawning. They have to be handled carefully and returned quickly to the water without damage. Later in the season, after the spring-run salmon, come the summer fish – grilse and, of course, the sea trout. East-coast rivers seem to have been less badly affected by the disastrous depletion of our sea trout stocks than the west-coast fisheries, and I can't help thinking that the dual aspects of fish farming and the intensive commercial sand-eel fishery are major factors in their demise.

The earliest sea trout sport I have had has been in saltwater in late February around the Island of Hoy and mainland Orkney. I travelled there one season for the opening, arriving back in time to meet up with Bill Currie on Beat 6 on the Helmsdale. Since I was travelling from Thurso by train, Bill picked me up at Kildonan, a few minutes from the beat. I had brought with me a brace of beautifully proportioned Orkney sea trout, the better fish comfortably topping 3 lb.

Bill had done better, a magnificent brace of sea-liced springers taken that morning, the later fish landed from the 'Vale of Tears' just minutes before my train had arrived. This was cause for celebration, and we called into the bar back in the village.

Competition between ghillies on any river is intense. But when you have two brothers vying for top honours on the same river, there is an added intensity to the competition.

'Strange, George,' I said, without making too much of the incident as I poured a dram into his glass. 'Both Bill and I have come back with a couple of fish apiece . . .' – word of Bill's two splendid springers had already reached the village – adding, '. . . But mine are sea trout.'

'Kelts . . . got to be in February,' George retorted unhesitatingly. 'I'd put a dram on it!'

A few minutes later George was examining the two sea trout in wide-eyed amazement, shaking his head slowly from side to side.

'Beauties, both of them . . . Never seen sea trout like that so early before!'

Neither had I – but I got my dram!

I'll call it 'The Rustle of Spring'. It really was a very long time ago – in fact, I was still at school, and our only form of salmon fishing in those days was Association water shared by characters whose integrity often varied as much as their skill. I'm afraid our own behaviour sometimes did little to endear us to the local bailiffs, whatever the river of our choice. I remember these early formative years with great affection, tinged with even greater embarrassment.

There was the time when we yearned for the wonderful stretch of lower Tay where the River Almond joins the main river opposite Scone Palace. Yes, of course I had a ticket; 5/- it had cost me and it was valid for the Perth Town Water. The fact that I had wandered a mile or so upstream (just for a look) and had then had a quick cast (or two) – well nobody had been looking. No harm was done really; a kelt returned to the water and another rod-bending snatch which could have been a springer. I escaped unharmed on that freezing January morning, and so did the fish.

Many years later I was a privileged guest of Jim Macfarlane, skilled angler and then proprietor of the Logierait Hotel, when we shared a day together on Almondmouth with the late Ken Balmain of Faskally. It was a memorable autumn day of 54 salmon landed, and a good number of ripe fish returned. Ken fished exclusively with the fly and took an impressive nine salmon to his own rod, including a

A youthful Mike Shepley on the Tay town water

tagged fish which he had personally released as a smolt into the River Almond some three years previously. He carefully measured and weighed the fresh-run salmon, and slipped it back. I'm sure there was a tear in his eye. My total was seven wild salmon, which remains my best single day's catch to date, although more recently I took 13 salmon from the River Lochy on fly one autumn day, but eight were farm escapees.

I digress. Let me return to the Tay of my youth more than 30 years ago. I didn't make it back to the North Inch the following week, but three chums did – on *my* day ticket. The day, date and name had been changed – smudged really, hopefully to protect the guilty!

No, of course they wouldn't venture upstream to the Grain Head – but they did. And caught a sea-liced springer. The bailiffs were not convinced that the salmon had come from the Town Water, and even less so that they 'were just having a look upstream'. The one grubby day ticket had been allocated to he who had caught the springer. Asked to produce their other permits, back came the reply, 'The one he's no' got will do the two of us!'

I never did fish the Town Water again, except for specimen roach and perch down at Perth Harbour. But that's another tale.

On Tweedside I got on well with both the local bailiffs, Bob Ritchie and Big Sandy. Bob even managed to obtain a local season ticket for me at a discounted price since I was still at school. We mostly caught kelts, although in those early years springers still ran Upper Tweed in March and April, and, given sufficient water, there were superb runs of salmon up the Ettrick. Indeed we also used to travel to Selkirk to watch the springers running the cauld in their hundreds. How times have changed.

Early one February, I hooked a largish fish at Cardrona, upstream from the railway bridge. Bob Ritchie and Big Sandy appeared as if by magic on the opposite bank. Thinking there might just be a chance that the salmon was clean, I ventured to cross the river so that the fish could be landed and examined by Bob and Sandy. In mid-river I lost my balance and went full tilt into the freezing stream. There was no such thing as waterproof or even water-resistant watches in those days, and my clothes were of the same ilk. I was soaked but . . . 'Hello *salar*.' My salmon was still on.

'It's a baggot!' said Sandy.

Bob Ritchie agreed. 'Got to go back, I'm afraid.'

'Looks all right to me.' My reply was tinged with plaintive hope. But then, I hadn't seen an unspawned over-wintered fish before. 'Pity,' I said, 'I've seen some fishers around here keep worse-conditioned kelts!'

One chap I'd heard even gutted his fish, cut them into steaks, packed them neatly into an assortment of reel pouches and stowed them casually around his large post-man's bag amongst other bits and pieces of tackle. Then it was off back to Edinburgh on the mid-morning train from Cardrona. Fortunately, the trains no longer stop at the station, and such behaviour is no longer tolerated. Quite rightly, such tricks have been eliminated and tickets terminated in no uncertain way.

Before I leave the early part of the season, I must briefly relate the story of my greatest number of salmon landed in a single day – 22 fish. While in numbers that February catch from the Tay beats the seven from Almondmouth and the 13 from the Lochy, most of the salmon were kelts and returned to the water.

I had 11 fish on a variety of spinning baits, devons, spoons and natural sprat. And 11 on the fly. Twenty were kelts and my 21st fish of the day was a magnificent springer of 17 lb. I also had an 18 lb baggot which was returned carefully to the water. Bill Currie and Lawrence Keith shared the day's sport with me, and between us we landed 56 salmon, all but the springer released, hopefully to make a successful return to saltwater.

MIDDLE CUT – THE SUMMER MONTHS

Early July, when the grilse runs are at their height, is perhaps my favourite time of the year for salmon fishing. These small 5- and 6-pounders fight spectacularly, often throwing themselves about the pools in cartwheels that send the adrenalin coursing through the veins. It is also a time of light tackle, small flies and the ubiquitous midge!

If there is one thing (or multitude of things) which I hate about summer, it is the nasty wee biters, blighters or any other names you want to call them. I remember almost crying and turning my back on a river full of salmon one such idyllic highland evening, spoilt by the presence of an army of the wee ***! Only someone who has experienced such anguish and pain – and that's only from the midge repellent – will understand my feelings. If they were bigger, I could at least have the satisfaction of swatting them.

Let's assume, though, that cloud-cover and a good breeze bless our arrival on the river bank. It will be early or late, for that is when the fish are most likely to take a fly. And besides, a game of golf on one of Scotland's splendid links courses is a much better proposition in the afternoon, when the day will be at its warmest.

Summer salmon fishing is a highly visual sport. The flies are tiny wisps of hair, the line is a floater, and the lure is either on or just sub-surface. When a fish rises to intercept the fly, the angler normally sees the salmon. It takes self-control not to strike too soon. Ideally, the fish should be allowed to take line directly from the reel, or the fisherman should hold a loop of line, allow the salmon to pull freely on the take, and only then raise the rod firmly to connect with the fish. Generally the result is positive, and the rod will arch to the pull of a well-hooked salmon.

If the fish takes the fly downstream and below the angler, the hook-hold might be more precarious. 'On the dangle' is our expression. You know too if the salmon

Eachaig delight for Mike

starts shaking its head like a dog worrying a bone, that it could well be hooked lightly in the front of the mouth rather than 'in the scissors'.

A feature of my salmon season in 1991, apart from lack of fish, was the size of the salmon and grilse. All the grilse were small; I had four between 2 lb 15 oz and 5 lb 2 oz. And my best salmon which came from the delightful Smithston Fishings on Ayrshire's River Doon was 10 lb 8 oz.

Sadly, I also lost quite a number of salmon this past season – bad news when chances come so few and far between. The ones that got away included a spectacular double on Beat 1 above, on the Helmsdale. I was fishing Duich Pool with ghillie Johnny Hardy, as a guest of Steve Bowler. The bright sunshine did nothing to suggest I would have much success. As is my preference for summer fishing, I had a number 8 double Munro on the dropper, and a double Silver Stoat a size larger on the tail.

Simultaneously, two grilse rose gracefully, one to each fly. I watched fascinated as they disappeared back down into the peaty depths, and then raised the rod. It was like lighting a fuse. The pool exploded in a cascade of white water, flashing flanks and frenzied fish. Both grilse were well and truly hooked, but I doubted if the 10 lb breaking-strain cast would hold for long. The speed at which the fish were charging about the pool gave the appearance of far more fish than two. Perhaps other salmon had been agitated by all the activity. The fun and anxiety lasted all of a minute. The cast didn't break as I had feared, but both grilse departed as they had appeared – together. It was a brilliant moment, unique in my experience as a salmon angler; little longer than a hiccup, but one which I shall never forget.

The smallest salmon I ever took was in 1961 on the Upper Oykel in Sutherland, where I spent long summer days ghillying on the river and Loch Ailsh, and occasionally walking the pony up Benmore Assynt trailing the stalker and guest guns out from the lodge. The grilse came from Sallachy Bridge Pool and weighed just 2 lb 10 oz.

The tiny salmon had taken the single-hook Jock Scott in a most unusual manner. I had seen the fish head-and-tail in the middle of the stream, right in the throat of the pool. Crouching down on the bank, I had cast a floating line and the number 6 fly pitched gently about 20 feet upstream from where I had seen the fish. Within seconds, the grilse appeared on the surface, mouth open, with the head clearly out of the water; the fly was still some feet upstream of the grilse, which held station as if treading water until the fly swam downstream to the waiting mouth. I could see the Jock Scott sucked in and the mouth close firmly as the

A maturer Mike Shepley

grilse slipped backwards under the surface. I waited two, perhaps three seconds, raised the rod and the fish was on. I've never had such an obliging salmon before or since.

Perhaps Oykel salmon are always generous to anglers. One woman, fishing the corner pool just below Loch Ailsh, had not quite mastered the timing of the cast, which generally ended with the lure being deposited in the middle of a guddle of fly-line and nylon cast. I watched from the high bank as a salmon rose through eight feet of water to untangle the fly neatly from the maze of line and take off down the pool. Safely netted by the ghillie ten minutes later, it was the lady's first-ever salmon.

Lord Thurso recounts a splendid tale relating to Her Majesty Queen Elizabeth, The Queen Mother. The Thurso River Superintendent, David Sinclair, was ghillying for Her Majesty on the Castle Pool when a large salmon was hooked and eventually brought to the waiting gaff. Skilfully, David took the salmon cleanly and swung it up the steep bank. Unfortunately, in so doing, the fish flew off the gaff in a final twist and kicked into the air back towards the river. As the salmon passed David for the second time in as many seconds, a quick flick of the gaff, and the salmon was once again secure, plucked from mid-air!

Her Majesty turned to the Superintendent: 'David, if I hadn't seen that myself, I would never have believed it!'

TAIL-PIECE – THE AUTUMN RUN

In 1922, the greatest Atlantic salmon ever to be caught in the British Isles was landed by Miss Georgina Ballantine, hooked *in Scotland* from the River Tay. It weighed 64 lb. A copy of the original photograph, kindly presented to me by the old tackle company, P. D. Malloch of Perth, suggests a rather more colourful cock fish than the imposing silvery specimen of the limited-edition cast one time on view at

Ballathie House, and more recently adorning a smoked salmon stall at Edinburgh Airport. I suspect for all its size, it would have smoked far better than the farm fish that make up the bulk of the commercial market these days.

I am not alone in saying that I have never ever hooked a salmon of such size. We all live in hope and trepidation of such a catch, but I fear the strain would be too much. I have witnessed the capture of a 44-pounder, though, a summer fish from Kinnaird on the River Tay. The same angler, again when I was present, played and eventually lost an enormous specimen on Mike Smith's beat, just above Dalguise Bridge. After nearly three hours, Bernard sadly decided he had had enough and tried to hold the unseen monster as it doggedly set off downstream. The link swivel broke and the fish was gone. Calum Gillies, who had originally ghillied on Kinnaird and had helped land the 44-pounder estimated this mighty Dalguise salmon as much larger.

'Ask the keeper about the "Sticks and Poos",' Paul Young had said, prior to my first visit to Delvine on the Lower Tay. It was early October and the river was full of fish. A pal who had never fished for salmon before had chummed me. I was confident he would have a better than even chance of success.

I wasn't over confident at asking anything about the 'poos', so I began by enquiring about the 'sticks'.

'Ah, well . . . those are the sticks across under the far bank,' explained the keeper, pointing to a tangle of shrub stumps which had encroached into the river on the eroded bank. 'Cast your Toby over there under the sticks, and that's where you get the poos!'

And so I did, first cast. I pulled a lively 10 lb cock salmon which was dispatched a few minutes later. It was 8.30 a.m.

Fish were splashing all over the pool, and while Jim wasn't quite reaching the 'sticks', he was getting the lure well out and it was fishing properly. I wasn't surprised when a yell brought me running back upstream where

Jim was playing a good fish, rod held well up and bent into a satisfying curve. 'Well done,' I said. 'Your first-ever salmon.'

Jim played the fish well, which surprisingly came quite quickly to the bank. A shallow gravelly area was ideal to beach the fish which broke surface. I couldn't believe my eyes. A river full of salmon, and Jim must have hooked the only pike for miles. They are found more often in the backwaters than the main river, but this 7-pounder was better out of the water. Never mind I thought, next time it will be a salmon.

I had landed three salmon by the time Jim's rod bent again. At least it wasn't another pike! The sea trout weighed 5 lb, a splendid fish for the Tay, but still not the salmon I had hoped for for Jim.

I had landed my best and last fish of the day – a 21-pounder. The keeper had joined me from the pool below, where he had also had success. As we chatted, an enormous salmon crashed out of the water, just yards from where we were standing.

'That has to be at least 45 lb!' I said.

'Bigger,' said the keeper.

I turned to see if Jim had also spotted the huge fish. He had. Jim's rod was bent at an alarming angle and line was ripping off his reel far too fast.

Off we went downstream until we were 200 yards from where the fish had been hooked. He showed twice more, and then headed out of the pool. A tree prevented us following, and we watched as the last of the line disappeared with a sickening crack.

'You pick your fish, Jim!' was all I could muster. It was a great disappointment for us all, but the keeper probably put the whole thing into perspective when he suggested that nobody could have landed such a fish from such a difficult pool without a boat to follow him downstream. It was the biggest salmon I've seen in my life.

My best-ever salmon was a much more modest cock fish

of 24 lb, taken from Norham in October on a small jungle-cock shrimp fly tube fished on a sink-tip line. I have hooked and lost similar-sized fish, all of them on Tweed. There was the 25-pounder (for that's my estimate) that followed my fly right to the bank on Upper Norham, and then swallowed it right at my feet before swimming slowly back into the depths. With the slack line, I was unable to tighten into the fish for nearly 10 seconds. I lost him after 45 minutes. Then, a little further upstream on the Junction Pool at Kelso, I was wading the left bank at Ednam House. Gordon on the boat didn't see me hook the large cock salmon which took off towards the bridge. Eventually the salmon tired, and I brought him into the shallows. I tried to work it over towards the garden wall, but the silty sand was too soft for my weight, and the water too deep. The big salmon was also too heavy to draw upstream to the island. I tried to tail him where I was, and had to tuck the rod under my arm to grasp the broad wrist with both hands. Halfway to the safety of the bank, my grip slipped and, at the same time, the fly fell out of the salmon's mouth. It rolled over twice and disappeared weakly back into the current.

Another autumn fish hooked at Scrogbank played strongly in heavy water for 15 minutes before I eased it into a backwater with the large kyped (hooked) head resting on a flat section of submerged bank. It was a classic autumn cock fish, deep-bodied, broad tailed and well into the 20s! I kept pressure on the line and the rod well bent as I worked down the bank to the exhausted salmon. I was no more than 20 feet from it when the fly sprung out of the corner of his mouth with a twang and embedded itself neatly in my hat! The salmon slipped backwards into the river and disappeared. I didn't actually *see* the fish go. In my mind's eye, what had slipped from my grasp were two sides of superb smoked salmon; I could almost smell the oaky flavour, the capers, freshly squeezed limes and ground black pepper.

But my story is not about *lost* salmon, so I won't detail the other disasters in my salmon fishing career – the fish hooked and lost with Joe below Kelso Bridge or the unseen salmon which I played at Norham for more than an hour. Both I'm confident were more than 30 lb – but they ain't landed, so they don't count! Neither does the monster which swirled at my black and orange bucktail tubefly one November under the arches of Norham Bridge. That was a seal!

Salmon fishing is about surprises, thrills, relaxation and, just occasionally, disappointment. Even when a fish is lost, the sadness seldom lasts for long. After all, the fish gained its freedom; that's all part of the game.

There are still rogues amongst fishermen; like the chap on lower Tweed below Kelso Bridge spinning a devon in December. I didn't see him; I had been watching salmon paired up for spawning on the gravel above the bridge, and had investigated a splash downstream. The salmon fortunately broke free, and shortly afterwards, when the devon sailed back out across the pool, I called down in my best bailiff's voice that not only had the season ended two weeks previously, but spinning on Tweed stops in the middle of September.

I thought back to my youth and chuckled. This surely wasn't someone who would go out at night with cymag poison or net or gaff. It was a preposterous gesture on any stretch of water, let alone one of the most exclusive stretches of salmon river in the country. It ranked with the cheek of a schooldays chum who once asked an angler to leave a stretch of Upper Tweed. 'Didn't he know this was a private beat?' – and then proceeded to fish without permission himself.

I do not condone such behaviour. I hope I enjoy my salmon fishing without detriment to the environment or to my fellow anglers. I return many of my late-season salmon to the water where practical, and encourage others to do the same. In these times of pressure both on our rivers and

Cheryl Pearce with a nice
autumn fish

the wild salmon, we all have a responsibility to ensure the survival of the Atlantic salmon, both as a natural resource and as part of our sporting legacy for future generations.

ADRIFT ON THE FACE OF THE WATERS

Stan Headley

Scotland is 'weel kent' as a country overflowing with potential for one of humanity's oldest passions, the pursuit of sporting fish as a pleasurable pastime. Salmon, sea trout and brown trout abound in the vast numbers of unspoilt rivers and lochs with which the nation is blessed, and it is virtually impossible to travel for an hour by car without passing some location or other which is renowned for its fishing potential. In a world where most industrial nations have pawned their heritage of ecological stability and wilderness, the treasure trove of Scottish trout and salmon waters is staggering and becomes more valuable as each day passes.

Whilst the average Jock in the street may not overly appreciate this wealth, thousands do, and each year they are joined by hordes of anglers, jaded by shoulder-to-shoulder fishing in the sometimes horribly artificial waters of the south. They come to Scottish shores to experience trout fishing as it should be and to tantalise their sporting taste buds with what we take for granted.

The Scottish rivers are the domain of the salmon and their devotees, to such an extent that in the past the caretakers of the rivers looked upon the brown trout as vermin to be exterminated. This somewhat suspect view is fast fading, and the present-day cost of salmon fishing, coupled with its sometimes dubious potential for supplying sport, has possibly turned the Land of King Salmon into the Republic of Trout. Our countryside is liberally bespeckled with lochs of all shapes, sizes and degrees of accessibility which are the accepted home of Scottish trout fishing. From the Borders to the Northern Isles there are standing bodies of water of every size and nature imaginable. Some are gigantic, deep and awesome, others, particularly in the Outer Isles, may be barely bigger than the average duck-pond. There are the forgotten tarns and lochans of the high hills, the glacial valleys with their awesome vastness and barbaric splendour, and the gentle lowland waters of the central belt which inevitably

Tactical discussion with Stan Headley

betray the application of man's hand. Many are so deeply stained with peat as to be stygian-black, whilst a comparable number have water so clear that it's hard to tell where the water stops and the air starts. Some are so remote as to be unreachable unless you have commando training, but others have trunk-roads running along their shores. There are trout lochs enough in Scotland to suit every taste, no matter how obscure – and the best part of it is that on most, and often the best, permission to fish is free for the asking.

No matter that the loch or lochan can be walked round in half an hour or that it stretches over the horizon, it is almost certainly home to the fish which, above all others, typifies fly fishing in its finest and fairest form. The brown trout of Scotland have captured the sporting mind for generations. Wherever fly fishermen gather to talk of the joys and qualities of their sport eventually Scottish trout will crop up in the conversation. In most branches of angling quality is synonymous with size – big and bigger fish are the objects of desire and attention. Not so with trout, however. Many fly fishermen have no hope from their local waters of a fish heavier than a supermarket bag of sugar and do not consider themselves in any way deprived. Such is the magic of loch fishing for trout. It is so much more than fishing and fish.

For hundreds of years people have gone in search of the spotted trout with rod, line and artificial flies. It has become a sport and pastime synonymous with peace, introspection, tranquillity and gentleness of spirit which belies the fact that it springs from our basic desire to hunt. The image of a man with a rod, either by the side of some picturesque remote water or adrift in a boat, is used by all sections of the media to portray a highly desirable state of being and is also a facet of a rapidly disappearing way of life. Who can deny that this is true?

Fly fishing for trout has an incredible ability to capture the imagination of its devotees. And, as with all incurable diseases, it leaves its mark for all to see. When your colleague suddenly goes glassy-eyed and remote as you pass the waterside, be it an effluent settlement lagoon or a picturesque Highland loch, you will know that, though he is with you in body, his spirit is far away where the trout swim. Other symptoms are manifested by the hopelessly addicted – restlessness and agitation with the onset of spring, a vague aroma of wetness and fish after holidays and weekends, sudden and unexected disappearances after phonecalls from locations with distinctly Celtic place-names, periodic attendances at the funerals of a host of relatives who require burial (often more than once!) by the side of trout lochs, and a predilection for old tweedy jackets festooned with ancient and redundant trout flies with exotic names like Greenwell's Glory, Grouse and Claret and Goat's Toe.

Is there any hope for the sufferer? Thankfully, no! But family and friends who may be worried over the social stigma of having ties with a terminal 'angler' can take hope. The major symptoms may be alleviated by large and regular doses of water in its natural state, interspersed with frequent rub-downs with fishing journals, continual application of praise and interest when fish are caught, sympathy when fish are not, and alcoholic stimulants at the close of day. Well, it works for me!

But before we go on, what of this magical fish which demands so much attention, devotion and love? The brown trout, or *Salmo trutta* as he is known to the scientists, is very much a fish of the northern reaches of Eurasia, although its natural range extends as far south as the Atlas Mountains of Africa. During the mid-19th century great efforts were made to introduce trout to various parts of the globe where they did not naturally occur. Now, Australia, New Zealand, South and North America, India and various parts of South Africa can be called home to trout. These exile populations exist because the sporting qualities of brown trout had become legendary, and no doubt the traveller, far from home, wished to take with him something intrinsically Scottish.

Surprisingly enough, given its popularity, your average brown trout is not normally a big fish. In the wild, only a few exceed a couple of pounds in weight, although those that do often stagger the imagination (Loch Stenness in Orkney produced a trout which weighed an almost unbelievable 29 lb!). But it is their verve, dash and willingness to come to the artificial fly that compensates for their sometime lack of size. Moreover, their colouring is another great attraction because, like fingerprints, no two trout are ever identical. If we take the famous Loch Leven fish – with their silvery background and sparse black spots – as one extreme of trout colouration, then their opposite must be the fish from the moorland tarns with their large black and red spots spread over a background of bronze and gold. And in between are almost every variation of colouring imaginable – black, brown, copper, gold and green backgrounds, some spots, no spots, orange fins, black fins. The important thing to remember, though, is that they are all *Salmo trutta*, the brown trout.

As a sporting fish, trout are justifiably renowned for being prolific in almost all their locations. The angler expects a fair amount of action whilst on the water and rarely goes out, like the salmon fisher, hoping for one massive fish which will keep him in free drinks at the bar for the rest of the week. Trout fishermen measure their catch in *baskets* – 'I had a good basket of fish from Loch Invercockyleekie!' or, 'When the mist is on the hill, and the haggis are singing their plaintive song, you can always rely on a basket from Loch Achnashug!'. But it is not simply the quantity of trout that attracts, it is also the fun they provide when hooked. Trout jump, sound, tail-walk, make the fly-reel scream in protest as they set off for pastures new, and they're never yours until safely in the net. I suppose, if asked, most time-served fly fishermen would tell you that the moment of magic is the 'take' – that frozen particle of time when the water erupts, a brief glimpse of spotted flank is seen, the rod bucks in the hand, the reel sings its special song, and suddenly it no longer matters that the rain is running down your back or into your sandwiches/cigarettes/socks, that the bank is about to foreclose, the baby needs new shoes, and the boss has been giving you that predatory look – you're into a fish, and isn't life great!

Sporting abilities apart, their appeal to the gourmet should not be forgotten. Brown trout which have a large proportion of their diet made up by crustaceans and molluscs (freshwater shrimp and snails) have the most succulent red flesh. Our local Orcadian fish have flesh of such a deep-red hue that they make even salmon look distinctly anaemic, and, although even pale pink trout flesh is eminently edible, the deeper the red the better it tastes. It comes from an organic colouring matter called, I believe, carotin, which is imparted by the crustaceans in their diet. Large quantities prove that the fish has been living 'high off the hog' and is packed with every vitamin, mineral and natural oil that you could want. This stuff is the epitome of health food!

Having said all that, though, like most life-long fishermen I must admit that my appetite for trout is not what it was, or should be. I suppose I've simply eaten too many over the years to get excited about them anymore, but there can be little doubt that, in the hands of a competent chef, trout can excite even the most jaded palate. My other half has a recipe for a starter which involves marinating carefully filleted slivers of *raw* trout in cream, lemon juice, spring onion, sugar and salt. I must admit, the idea of eating raw trout took a bit of getting used to (having no Japanese element in my ancestry), but it tastes wonderful. Indeed, funnily enough, given my failing appetite for trout, when the very first new potatoes arrive on the market, I start to hanker for a few fillets, fried in bacon fat, coupled with the new spuds, smothered in a heap of fresh green peas and washed down with a good Chablis. Divine!

And isn't it a joy to come home from a hard day's grafting on the water and have the fruits of your effort appreciated. My wife has always tolerated my passion for fishing – but if I was addicted to the pursuit of some totally inedible species, perhaps her patience would have worn a trifle thin by now. Of course, you don't have to eat the brutes yourself. They make great items of barter. I have an unfortunate allergy towards all things horticultural, but I get my fair share of organic veg from grateful recipients of trout. And even if the beneficiary of your largesse can't stand gardening either, there are boundless possibilities for repayment of fishy favours – like babysitters, dog-minders, technical assistance with jobs around the house . . . Yes, a trout in the hand is worth a lot of goodwill, but never forget that a fish returned to the water may safeguard endangered populations in hard-fished waters!

Modern advances in technology have helped to improve the lot of the angler. Space-age materials such as carbon, boron and kevlar have produced fishing tackle capable of being used all day without severe pain ensuing. It never ceases to amaze me that at the age of ten I fished with a cast-off split-cane rod that had belonged to my father. Admittedly, I was not able to fish continuously for long periods with it but, if I was forced to wield such a weapon now, I'd end up with either a wrecked shoulder or a hernia – and probably both. These days, when after a long stint my $3\frac{5}{8}$ oz, 11-foot fly rod starts to feel somewhat cumbersome, I think back some 30 years and bless the miracles of technology. And it is not only in the field of rod construction that advances have been made. We now have monofilament nylon for leader construction which is ridiculously strong given its lack of bulk. And hooks are now available which are, to all intents and purposes, totally corrosion resistant and capable of lasting for as yet unquantifiable periods of time with little or no attention.

As the pull of the wild places increases in this age of

hi-tech urbanisation, and more and more people succumb to the lure of fishing as a means of shaking off the shackles of modern-day stresses and strains, it is perhaps as well that the sources of the said pressure are capable of helping us stay one step ahead of the increasing sophistication of trout. On hard-fished waters trout do become wary of the angler's approaches, but we have no means of assessing whether this is an instinctive process or learning from experience. We do know that, in human terms, trout are simple creatures with little or no ability to reason. Reacting to their environment in purely instinctive ways, it is entirely possible that they are totally oblivious to the existence of humanity. I personally find this frustrating. After all, most dedicated trout men spend large amounts of spare time either hunting them, thinking up ways to better tackle the wee devils, preparing for the next foray, or simply mulling over past victories or failures – and all the while the object of our efforts and passions is blissfully unaware that we exist. Unfeeling brutes! Mind you, I sometimes bless this state of affairs because I am tormented by an irrational fear that some day a Messiah amongst trout is going to appear and say, 'Hey! Wait just a minute', put two and two together, slip on his open-toed sandals, pick up his staff, and set out on a great mission of redemption and salvation for his spotted brethren – and that, as they say, will be that!

But until that day dawns, we trout fishermen will endeavour to take our annual harvest from the lochs. The boats will set out in the mornings to drift upon the face of the waters. The rods will flicker backwards and forwards, the flies will swim and dance, the unsuspecting trout will rise and plunge, and all will be well with the world. To be out in a boat with a friend, with no thoughts intruding bar those concerned with fish and fishing develops an inner peace unknown in other leisure activities. And the secret is in the camaraderie.

It has been said that a greater degree of circumspection is required in selecting a boat-partner than in selecting a

*Stan Headley – a fine, well-
organised angler*

wife. Brave words! Having no wish to discover ground glass in my sandwiches or strychnine in my thermos flask, I totally refute this suggestion. But there is an element of truth in the assertion that incompatible boat-partners can turn paradise into purgatory. I well remember an occasion on Loch Leven's pier when those there assembled witnessed a harrowing sight. A boat approaching the dock, bearing three anglers, was seen to be weaving an erratic course home. On closer appraisal, it was obvious that the anglers were involved in serious altercation. The two anglers in the fore section of the boat were indulging in the ancient art of fisticuffs with little regard to the Marquis of Queensberry's instructions, whilst the chap in charge of the motor was either endeavouring to instil a degree of calm on the situation or was offering advice as where next to land the telling blow, with little regard to steering. They managed to come alongside the pier with some difficulty, at which point the losing assailant ended up in the water. In fairness, it should be noted that this occurred during a competition which had involved boat placings being 'drawn from a hat' and the altercation was not the termination of a lifelong friendship. Such experiences are rare, though, and in 30 years of fishing it is the only example of its type known to me.

Much more common are friendships of duration and strength born from first-time meetings in boats. I wonder if it is an admission of inadequacy that most of my best friends are my fishing partners. But there can be little doubt that the ability to spend whole days in close confinement with another individual whilst indulging in an activity which throws at one the whole gamut of emotions, forges friendships against which the troubles of the world crumble to dust. To be able to congratulate your partner on the capture of his tenth trout whilst waiting impatiently for your first requires a breadth of spirit and character rare in other fields of human endeavour.

Good fortune in fishing can be most contrary – visiting

Posers! Two past Scottish National Champions

one end of the boat and totally deserting the other, or
bounteously endowing one angler whilst leaving his friend
bereft and desolate. When I won the Scottish National
Fly Fishing Championship of 1990 on Loch Leven, I caught
eight fish whilst my unfortunate partner, who shall remain
nameless as the scars are still fresh, failed to boat a single
fish. A fishing friend of long-standing also took part in this
competition. His tale was almost as harrowing. In the
dying minutes of the match, he hooked an enormous fish –
the fish of a lifetime – but, due to the necessity of being
back at the pier within the time allowed, was forced to
apply an excessive amount of bullying tactics to subdue
the leviathan. Of course, the inevitable happened and he
lost the uncaring brute, and when poor Sandy arrived
at the weigh-in his face was tripping him. Believe it or
believe it not, both these unfortunate experiences of others
spoiled the euphoria to which I was entitled on becoming
Scottish Champion. Most fishermen will admit that their
own victories are augmented when their friends are like-
wise blessed. There is little joy in being the only recipient
of good fortune. Much better to be numbered amongst a
group of happy anglers sipping the amber nectar in celebration, than to be the only happy face amongst a crowd of
sorrow-drowners.

Don't think for one moment that I am promoting my luck
as steadfast and sure, for that would be a lie. I once spent
an evening fishing with a chap from Bridge of Weir. He
confessed to being a novice in the gentle art, and admitted
that his meagre experience had been gleaned from artificial
waters containing rainbow trout. He was keen to learn and
I offered advice on how to improve his tackle and choice of
fly pattern to better deal with sophisticated 'brownies'. He
promised to follow my advice at a later date, but felt that he
had better stick to what he knew for the time being. Fearing
the worst for him, I prepared myself to console the poor
chap at the end of the day. He left the water with a basket
of trout which would gladden the heart of any experienced

fisherman – whilst I was forced to content myself with the couple of escapees from a sardine can. Fishing can be excessively cruel at times!

The observant amongst you may have noticed that I have continually referred to fishing for trout as 'fly fishing'. This may confuse non-anglers as the layman's conception of fishing in general involves a myriad of irrelevances including umbrellas, stools, rod-rests and bait. We can only blame the media for this wide-spread misconception of fishing, particularly when applied to trout. Admittedly, bait, or more accurately, the ubiquitous worm, has played a historical part in trout fishing. But as the years pass, the number of anglers who prefer to take their fish with artificial fly increases apace.

Trout 'flies' are in themselves a fascinating subject. And although there are a minority of fly-fishermen who couldn't tell a Grouse and Claret from a slap-up feed, most self-respecting anglers take great pride in their knowledge of artificial flies – their history, their proper place in the scheme of things, and when and where best to employ them. Scotland has always been at the forefront of the development of fly-tying as an art, and has spawned quite a number of fur and feather creations which are famed throughout the world as reliable takers of trout – Peter Ross, Ke-He, Loch Ordie, Black Pennel, Dunkeld, and the previously mentioned Grouse and Claret all claim Scottish descent and have served the cause of fly fishing for gene-erations. Tied (one does not make a trout fly, one *ties* it) to vaguely represent items of trout fare, they are remarkably successful although, to the doubting eye, they certainly don't have any resemblance to real flies living or dead. Bright and garish or sombre and subtle, artificial flies are a large factor in the appeal of fly fishing and, when the winter months drive the fishermen from the lochs, temporary solace can be obtained by a brief jaunt down memory lane via the tidying-up of fly-boxes.

Greater solace and satisfaction is obtainable, however, to the fisherman who can tie his own flies and pass the weary winter months beavering away at the fly-tying bench surrounded by fur, feather, silk and tinsel, and breathing in the heady fumes of moth-balls and varnish. The art of fly-tying has increased in popularity tremendously in the past decade (probably due to the encouragement of the fishing journals) and the skilled amateur fly-dresser can produce either the standard, time-served patterns or, by the application of inspiration and experience, create his own killers. The art is limited only by the individual's imagination and the resources of his fly-tying kit. Not that every product of the fertile mind will prove a successful fly. Far from it! But the ability to produce one's own trout flies can provide one

A moody evening to be afloat

of fishing's greatest thrills – to create something out of nothing with one's own hands, and with it to catch yesterday's uncatchable fish. I am also a firm believer that the ability to 'roll your own' encourages a more thoughtful and enquiring fishing mind, and consequently a more adept practitioner of the angling art.

I was very young when I tied my first trout fly, probably about 13 years old. But I can remember to this day the colours and construction of it, and even more vivid in my memory is the trout which engulfed it. I was fishing in a very deep, disused and flooded stone-quarry into which trout had been introduced many years before. The trout were of admirable size but, due to their inability to reproduce in this environment (trout normally require running water in order to spawn successfully), were a bit thin on the ground. My normal fishing method in those dim and distant days was to indulge in a bit of worm drowning. But, having begun my apprenticeship in the intricate art of fly-dressing, I was tempted to try one of my new creations, more in hope than expectation I must admit. At one point, when the fly had sunk to a considerable depth due, probably, to my youthful lack of attention, it was taken by a trout with suicidal determination. The picture in my mind of that fish, all golden, shiny, and as mad as hell, erupting from the water like a polaris missile and surrounded by a halo of sunlit spray, remains fresh to this day. And at that fateful moment a *fly*-fisherman was born! Unfortunately, some years ago the local council filled in the birthplace of my passion and it is now simply the corner of a field. But every time I pass the place I mentally doff my cap to that day, that first fly-caught trout and the long-gone birthplace of so much pleasure and joyful experience. I owe it more than I can say!

From such mundane surroundings the sport of fly-fishing has taken me to some of the most attractive places in this country. I have seen the sun strike sparks from the grey sides of Bienn Mhor and Hecla in South Uist whilst

It seemed a monster at the time. A trout from the Tighnabruaich burn

Denis 'The Hat' Lennox

Two fine Helmsdale springers.
One fine Helmsdale raincoat

Ted Zawadzki, 'Towser' Lowe,
Johnnie MacDonald and
Sartorial Disaster

Sunsets are often spectacular out on the Forth

Friedrik makes a head count of the Arctic char

Helmsdale spring snowflakes. It's great fun . . . honest!

Mike Shepley casting a line on the Lyon

The record Stenness trout

Afloat on a South Uist machair loch

Part of the Howmore system on South Uist

A fresh Lower Kildonan sea trout

the trout struck at the fly with primordial savagery, encouraged by the corncrakes calling from the machair. I have seen aquatic flies rise in their millions, their massed wings making the air shake in resonance, as they danced their nuptial dance over Castle Island on Loch Leven, where poor Mary Queen of Scots pined away her bleak incarceration. I have heard the mournful wail of the red-throated divers sounding over Loch Swannay in Orkney, heralding the long-awaited rain (it is no coincidence that they are known locally as 'rain geese'), and the arctic terns screaming defiance as the boat drifts ever closer to their island homes on Loch Harray.

The trout fisherman at large on the lochs of Scotland is in perpetual contact with nature in the raw. Try as he might, there is no ignoring the fact that all around him is the continual movement and sensation of the natural world. Spring is a sensual cacophony which delights and invigo-rates the angler – the scent of mint, the colours of the wetland orchids, the merry dance of the bog-cotton, the drumming of snipe, lapwings crying and dragging their 'broken' wings in that age-old ritual of deceit, invisible ring plovers and sandpipers calling from the gravelly bays and the ducks with their brood, line-astern, running the gaunt-let of hungry skuas and black-backed gulls.

Summer is more somnolent and subdued but with its own special magic. The pretty pond olives drift, wings vertical, like sailing boats over the water, or lift in the breeze to be picked-off with pretty precision by the terns and blackheaded gulls in one of nature's most graceful ballets. The never-tiring swifts swoop and weave high over the water, intercepting the flies trapped in the thermals, and the mother otter whistles to her straying cubs. The scent of meadowsweet and freshly-turned hay spices the breeze, the bedlam of the gull and tern nesting-colonies assaults the ears, and the variations of green befuddle the counting eye in a landscape sucking up the sunshine and the infrequent showers of rain.

Then nature shakes off her mid-year slumbers, and autumn is with us. The summer bird populations disperse and the wild geese, the hounds of heaven, fill the skies with their skeins and cackling call. Grouse croak warningly as the boat encroaches upon the heather-clad shoreline, the stags roar defiance across the moor, and duck explode alarmingly from the reed-choked bays. Daddy-longlegs tumble end over end before the sudden squall of wind, trying to lift themselves from the water, only to disappear for ever in the mad, slashing rise of the trout. Caddis flies, more at home on the water, scuttle energetically shorewards to the haven of bankside vegetation. Mauves, purples and reds splash across the heather hillsides, and yellows, browns and every shade in between supersede the greens of the agricultural fields.

And then the fishing season draws to a close and the lochs are deserted by the fisherman. Under the leaden skies of winter the waters look grey and uninviting, but below the surface life goes on. Most of the fish will remain in the lochs throughout the winter months, reducing their activity and conserving energy, patiently awaiting the birth of spring and the burgeoning of life that accompanies it. Many, however, will enter the burns and feeder streams – some never to return to the lochs – in order to spawn and thus produce the next generation of trout in the continuing drama of life, death and rebirth which epitomises nature.

I suppose there are fly fishermen who dread the close season and fret and fidget their way through the winter months. I personally take it in my stride and use the time to catch up on things sadly neglected through the summer. Fly-tying, tackle renovation and rejuvenation, re-reading the previous summer's fishing magazines and catching up with new thinking and trends in fishing technique consume large quantities of time and are better attempted when the mind is fresh with a hunger for fishing sharpened by abstinence. There is also the vitally important task of reintroducing myself to my family – 'Hello! Remember me?

I'm your dad!', or even more ticklish, 'Nice doggy, good doggy! My, what a sharp set of teeth!'

Regardless of the pitfalls which are part and parcel of every fisherman's life, we in Scotland are blessed indeed! Not for us the petty bureaucracy, commercialism and artificiality of the English reservoir or pond. No shoulder-to-shoulder stuff, or arguments about who was where first! Little danger of collision with motor boat, cabin cruiser or sailboard run amok, and only out of choice need the angler return with a collection of tailless, finless refugees from a restaurant freezer! Scotland retains a large slice of the western world's rapidly disappearing wilderness. Our birthright of mountain and moorland, loch and river is resistant to change, urbanisation and all that destroys and debases. Much of what we see today is as it always was and should be. And to the fly-fisherman in pursuit of wild trout, Scotland is a paradise of plenty, a haven of peace and tranquillity, a retreat from the madness of 20th-century life. Long may it remain so.

SEA TROUT YOU'LL GET UIST TO

John Kennedy

This suggestion of the sea and of the migratory fish is one of the charms of Island angling . . . in fishing any Hebridean loch of this type, one always feels assured that sea trout are there to see . . . on Lower Kildonan or Roag, a sea trout seems the capture proper to the water . . . hence hope never suffers the arm to tire when casting in the waters of the west.

Book of the Sea Trout,
Hamish Stuart, 1917

Anyone who has fished the waters of South Uist would agree with those sentiments, even though they were written so long ago. South Uist is an angler's paradise with men and women coming from all over the world to tackle the famous machair lochs of the western seaboard which contain some of the finest wild brown trout in the country. Grilse and salmon are also an attraction in their own right but, to top them all, we have sea trout. The sea trout runs on the west side of Scotland in particular have suffered almost to the point of extinction in some places in recent years, but the fish are still plentiful on South Uist and hundreds are caught in a relatively short season from mid-July to the end of October. This came about some years ago when it was obvious that more and more salmon were being caught each year in what were almost pure sea trout systems.

John Kennedy – South Uist expert

Salmon are later spawners, and we were aware of the damage and disturbance that they can cause to the earlier-formed redds of the sea trout. However, we decided to try to live with both species. In 1984 we began an ongoing programme of introducing gravel to extend existing redds and creating new ones where necessary – and indeed possible. We also started stocking sea trout fry from time to time but, rightly or wrongly, we feel that looking after the environment and the habitat of the sea trout will produce better results than stocking ever will.

Anyway, sea trout run big on South Uist with the average fish coming in at around 2.8 lb. Every fish under 1½ lb is returned carefully to the water and, with finnock not killed as a rule, fish of more than 5 lb are common while 10 lb fish are certainly not rare.

As an Ayrshire lad, I caught sea trout from the Doon and Nith and in later life have fished as far afield as the Falkland Islands and the North and South Esk. But, even allowing for bias, I'm bound to say that, for sheer quality, the sea trout from the west coast of South Uist take a lot of beating. A 5 lb fresh-run fish from Lower Kildonan, for example, is as fine a specimen of sea trout as you are ever likely to see. Not even the Falklands, productive as they are, can compare.

I went to the Falklands as a quartermaster of a logistics battalion responsible for the resupply of the garrison after the Falklands conflict. I had hoped that I would get some time to fish in my six months on the islands and by the end of my stay had fished three rivers, all in East Falkland.

For me the most striking feature of the islands was their similarity to South Uist in terms of the local terrain. The Murrell River, west of Port Stanley, is probably the least-known river on the islands but for me it was the most accessible – a relative concept since it still involved a four-hour round trip on foot through some pretty rough peat-bog country. That could also explain why, next to my rod, my camera was the most important part of my equipment.

It was better to photograph the fish and return them than carry them back across miles and miles of land like that.

I was also lucky enough to manage a couple of trips by helicopter to fish the San Carlos River, a very abundant sea trout river on the west side of the island. On one journey I noticed that the top section of my rod had broken off on the flight. Anyway, with five hours to kill, a little doctoring and trimming with my pen-knife produced a makeshift rod with which I managed to catch five sea trout, the best I think around 9 lb.

I only had one successful but embarrassing visit to the famous Malo River – successful because I caught four sea trout, one of them weighing in at 13 lb. The embarrassment came at the end of the day when I discovered I had been fishing on private water. Needless to say, I didn't return there.

But let us leave the South Atlantic behind and return to South Uist. Almost every freshwater outlet on the island has a run of sea trout, but, generally speaking, the best are to be found in the west-coast systems. The two main ones are the Kildonan-Mill system, which consists of Lower Kildonan Loch, Mill Loch and Upper Mill Loch and the Howmore River system, comprising Loch Roag and Loch Fada to the south, and Schoolhouse Loch and Castle Loch to the north.

Neither system requires spate conditions to entice fish. In the case of the Howmore, spring tides push right up this short tidal river, rushing through the culverts under the road and into Loch Roag. On some occasions the tides have even been known to go from Loch Roag to Loch Fada with which it has an excellent connection, while the same also applies to Schoolhouse Loch but to a lesser extent. Although the tide does not reach the loch itself, the north arm of the river can cause the burn which descends from the Schoolhouse to back up, leaving the fish to spill into the pool beneath and run the ebbing brackish water.

The Kildonan system is unique because the last 60 metres

of the Roglas burn, which drains it into the Atlantic, runs underground and extends some 30 metres into the sea through a concrete tunnel. The tunnel has been in existence since the turn of the century and it would appear to have been built to prevent a build-up of seaweed blocking the burn's relatively narrow outlet. At high tide the tunnel is covered by the sea and the descending fresh water again backs up the Roglas Burn almost as far as the loch, once more enabling the fish to run the brackish water at the turn of the tide.

Of course, having said initially that neither system requires spate conditions to enable the fish to run, there is no substitute for rain. In a perfect world a good downpour every two weeks throughout the season to coincide with the spring tides would enable fish to spread through the systems at will.

LOCH ROAG

Roag is arguably the most prolific loch on South Uist in terms of its total catch. Almost oval in shape, it is less attractive than some of the other lochs, but on its day it can be tremendous. Curiously, its main asset – being able to get a run of fish straight off the tide in low-water conditions – is also a major drawback in terms of fishing conditions. During the spring tides the tide will make the loch twice daily and, if there is not enough fresh water coming in from the hill burn, the loch becomes very salty. The fish will still be there but will be difficult to take for a day or two at least. The record sea trout for the island used to be a 14 lb hen fish, taken here in 1965 by Rupert Ponsonby with a size 8 Black Pennel. The record stood until 1991 when, again on this loch, I took a fresh-run hen sea trout of 14 lb 6 oz on a size 8 Green French Partridge.

LOCH FADA

This is the sister to Loch Roag, connected by a short burn that runs under a secondary road. It is a pleasure to fish with Hecla and Ben Mohr, the two highest peaks on the island, providing a stunning backdrop. One of its great attractions is that, even in high winds when you would never consider taking a boat out, it remains fishable from the bank. The burn mouth on Loch Fada is legendary. It is a narrow rocky bay, where, in spate conditions, the main spawning burn will thunder into the loch on the north-east shore with such force that the water almost reaches the opposite bank. It is a great spot to see fish show and jump and the only place on the loch to have lunch. My idea of paradise on earth is to sit behind one of the old ruins at the burn mouth on the Fada, with a flask and a sandwich, watching the gale-force winds driving the horizontal rain all the way to the mist-shrouded hills far in the distance.

SCHOOLHOUSE LOCH

Although it is part of the same system, Schoolhouse is very different from Roag and Fada. Schoolhouse, like Castle, is gin-clear while the other two are peat stained and even at their best resemble cold tea. Both Roag and Fada are fed by spate burns that rush straight into them after crossing peaty moorland. In contrast, the spawning burn which feeds Schoolhouse – and Castle with which it is connected – has its water filtered through Loch Druidibeg, a national nature reserve and one of the biggest freshwater lochs on the island. By the time the water reaches Castle Loch it is clear of peat but the contrast becomes really obvious when, having left Schoolhouse, it merges at the junction of the Howmore River with the peat-tainted water from Roag and Fada.

Schoolhouse is a difficult little loch to fish but it can be very rewarding. Indeed, although it is a one-boat loch, it actually has two – the loch being divided into two arms – north and south. In low-water conditions a series of stepping stones and a small bridge across the stream means it is difficult to manoeuvre a boat between the two arms. The only way to get round this is to have a boat on each arm which are then fished in rotation. The idea is that you select the most likely arm, give it two or three drifts, rest up, change boats and try the other one. However, because of the clear water and the small surface area to be fished, it is sometimes wiser, if the wind conditions permit, to give it a try from the bank before you even consider taking the boat out. It is a long time since a double-figure fish came out of Schoolhouse – hardly surprising given its degree of difficulty. It does, nonetheless, give up its fair share of 5–7 lb sea trout every season, and being deep, trout can be taken almost anywhere providing it is fished quietly and carefully. A gem of a loch.

CASTLE LOCH

Similar to Schoolhouse but much larger, Castle Loch is one of the better places to take fresh-run sea trout later in the season – say from mid-September through October. The large island on the west side of the loch contains the ruins of the castle which gives the water its name. This was reputedly a prison at one time and there is a certain amount of local superstition surrounding the loch and its eerie backdrop.

Again, like Schoolhouse, large fish are seen but seldom caught. Castle also holds a large head of wild brown trout averaging around the ¾ lb mark which can still make for an interesting day's fishing when their migratory cousins are not responding. I like to stress to visiting anglers that, due in part to the clarity of the water, this very interesting and under-rated loch should be fished with care but optimism. The sea trout are always there and are of good quality and size if you can forget the ghosts.

LOWER KILDONAN

Even though it does not hold the same head of sea trout as those lochs which make up the Howmore River system, this is, in my opinion, the jewel of the South Uist sea trout lochs. There is a certain attraction in fishing this incomparable loch. For me, a 4 lb sea trout hooked and successfully landed from Lower Kildonan is worth one twice its weight from any other water. What makes it so special is its size

A brace of Machair brown trout

and depth, and the difficulty in playing and landing a fish. The loch is extremely shallow – about 4 feet all round – and is surrounded by reed-beds which can give the angler some heart-stopping moments as he tries to keep a large sea trout away from them and possible disaster. I recall a father and son a few years ago having fished Lower Kildonan all day and returning to the hotel empty handed and on the point of tears. Between them they had managed to hook and lose – mostly to the reed-beds – five good sea trout and a salmon. We never saw them again. On the other hand, one of the nicest, most perfectly-formed sea trout I have ever seen came off this loch in 1989. It weighed in at 10½ lb, was fresh run and the angler, London barrister Patrick Back, celebrated his birthday that evening in fine style. Because of its size and depth, Lower Kildonan is fishable all over and wherever you fish you can always expect something to happen, which is seldom the case on any other loch.

MILL LOCH

Undoubtedly the most difficult loch on the island. In spate conditions I have seen dozens of fish packing the burn mouth on Lower Kildonan to make their way the 150 yards to Mill Loch but when they get there they simply seem to vanish. Mill Loch is certainly a lot bigger and deeper than Kildonan, which means the fish can spread out and are harder to catch. Nonetheless, it can drive sane men – and even ghillies – to despair.

It is a fascinating loch. In the 1991 season local ghillie John Gray was fishing the loch with two Londoners. The Mill was as dour as usual until a fish finally took the fly of the stern rod. It rolled once before taking off and everyone could see it was obviously a big one. In its initial run the fish took the whole line, backing off the reel and broke the cast above the fly. Once things had calmed down all three men went ashore to assess the damage. Pacing it out on the bank the angler found that he had 140 yards of line and backing and, even allowing for John rowing hard after the fish, it was not enough. Some people laugh at me when I tell them my reel takes 250 yards of backing but in a loch where there are big sea trout and salmon about you may need it.

The Mill Loch is a challenge. The fish are not as free-rising as in some other lochs which leads some to suspect there are none there at all. But if you come along in late October and have a look at the fish ascending the burn to the Upper Mill, you could almost walk across their backs.

UPPER MILL

Although boats generally do not go out on the Upper Mill until well into the season around early September, it can outfish the Mill Loch earlier in the season if conditions are good, with perhaps unseasonal torrential rain in late July or early August.

For reasons best known to themselves, some sea trout and salmon will run as far as conditions will allow when they first enter fresh water. It never ceases to amaze me that, in a system such as this – with three lochs and more than three miles of spawning burn as the headwater – fresh fish can be caught in the top loch as early as July, yet in late October stale and gravid ones can be taken in the bottom one. Indeed, this is still the case even in the wettest of summers when the fish have every opportunity to advance up the system but choose not to. The loch does not feature on the hotel fishing rota and is therefore not classed as a beat loch but more as an extension to the Mill Loch. Anglers who have fished the Mill can, if they wish, take a short walk up the adjoining burn between the lochs and enjoy the change of scenery with the chance of a good fish. It is not unknown for anglers to blank on Mill Loch but score on Upper Mill, particularly when conditions are right and there is a good flow of water entering the head of the loch from the Hornary River, the main spawning burn for the whole system.

So, the fishing in South Uist is at present in a healthy state and anglers come back year after year to sample the delights of angling for wild fish in wonderful country.

Come in May or June for the Machair brown trout and July to October for the sea trout and salmon. If the weather is kind, giving good water conditions, you may have a fishing holiday to remember and even if the fishing is challenging, the memory of a 2 lb machair brownie or 4 lb pound fresh run Lower Kildonan sea trout will bring you to South Uist time and again. Then there are the salmon!

We look forward to welcoming you to Lochboisdale.

RAINBOWS OVER SCOTLAND

Brian Peterson

With so many Scottish rivers and lochs teeming with wild brown trout, it might seem strange that someone felt it necessary to stock them with rainbow trout. It seems to have been done for reasons of economy and variety; economy because rainbows are cheaper than brown trout, and variety because anglers appeared to want to fish for a larger species of trout.

The Howietoun Fishery near Stirling was one of two UK hatcheries into which rainbows were first introduced from the United States back in 1885. The first water to be stocked was Blagdon Water near Bristol. That was in 1904, and by the 1970s well over 500 waters throughout the UK had been stocked with the fish. There are two different strains of rainbow – migratory and non-migratory – with Scottish waters mainly stocked with the migratory variety. The first Scottish waters to experiment with this new species were places like the Lake of Menteith, Loch Fitty and Butterstone Loch. As the reputation of these hard-fighting rainbow trout grew, anglers started to flock to those waters which had prudently stocked them. I say prudent because the majority of waters which put rainbows in were leased by angling clubs who were looking for a cheaper way to increase their stocks of fish.

The lifespan of a rainbow trout is about four or five years but it was found to put on weight rapidly which suited both the breeder and the angler. There was intense rivalry between the different waters to see who could produce the heaviest fish. This in turn led to the introduction of the jumbo trout, with the Lake of Menteith the first to take the plunge in this particular field.

With heavier, more combative fish came a whole new range of tackle for those who wanted to pursue them. Rods had to change from the supple soft action to a stiff poker to throw out a fast-sinking WF9, a shooting head, or even a lead core to get way down to the depths in cold weather. Lines changed too. Gone were the floater and the sinker, to be replaced with the strange-sounding High Floater, Wet Cel 1, Wet Cel 2, Intermediate, Fast Sinker, Ultra-fast Sinker, Hi-D, Lead Core and so on. Then came novelties

Brian with a good still-water rainbow

like braided leaders and 25-foot casts. But if all of these were new and bewildering, there was more in store when it came to the question of lures.

Strange names started to appear on the lips of Scottish anglers who suddenly found themselves discussing the relative merits of the Ace of Spades versus the Cat's Whisker, or the Appetiser, or a Jack Frost, or even a Leprechaun. Then there was the infamous Dog Nobbler which, when tied, incorporated a small piece of lead at the head. This frequently meant it took on a life of its own when it was cast and for a time produced a rise in demand for protective glasses and headgear. It could end up in the most peculiar places and even, occasionally, in a fish. However, the Dog Nobbler's saving grace is that it is a most effective lure for browns as well as rainbows.

Thankfully, anglers also discovered that rainbows could be taken on small traditional wets, dries and small buzzers. Flies like the Soldier Palmer were probably the most effective, although it could be tied in many forms, as happens with a lot of traditional patterns these days. The Cat's Whisker, which I mentioned earlier, is also very popular. It incorporates two of the most frequently used materials in tying rainbow lures; marabou and chenille. However, there are many variations, and some incorporate that other widely used material, pearl lurex, which produces many different colours depending on the pattern in which it is tied.

My own favourite, though, is a small lure called the Lawfield Nobbler which was named after a small water fishery at Kilmacolm. It is tied as follows:

hook, 10 or 12 normal or longshank;

tail, orange marabou;

body, fluorescent yellow chenille, palmered with a hot orange cock hackle;

head, a lead-substitute shot varnished black with a white eye painted on.

I have found it most successful when fished on a single fly cast of around 11 feet on a floating line. A very slow retrieve, even as slow as a figure of eight, seems to have the best effect. It also works well with a small nymph about six or seven feet up the cast.

On the other hand, another successful variety includes a small muddler about eight feet from the cast so that the muddler stays on the surface for a while. You should also bear in mind the variations which can be tied. Try a Cat's Whisker without lead, which is particularly good if you don't want it to sink so quickly. I remember introducing Paul to the original Cat's Whisker on the Lake of Menteith – at which point he promptly began to empty it of rainbow trout. I think you could safely say he was convinced of its effectiveness. (*Sure was! Paul.*)

The introduction of rainbow trout also led to a sharp rise in popularity for the nymph, which had been seldom used up until then. The most popular are the Montana and the Pheasant Tail which both come in various colours of thorax. The Damsel is also very successful, especially at times when the damsel flies can be seen flitting across the surface of the water, dipping their tails in as they lay their eggs. The trout usually take the nymph just under the surface so the best method is to use a floating line or a sink-tip line with a fairly long leader to be cast out and left for a while to allow it to sink. A lot of fish will prefer to take the nymph as it is sinking towards the bottom, so once you have decided that your nymph is at the required depth, it should be retrieved slowly – again, you might try a figure of eight. This involves retrieving the line with one hand in a figure-of-eight movement. It has proved popular and, although it requires practice and a certain amount of patience, the effort can be well rewarded.

On the subject of nymphs, I must mention the Booby which has become an established and popular method of luring the reluctant rainbow out of the depths. It has a tail of marabou plumes and the body is chenille, ribbed with

silver or gold wire. It takes its name from the final part of
the tying which incorporates two polystyrene balls wrap-
ped in a small piece of ladies' tights and tied in at the eye of
the hook. You can imagine for yourself what the finished
product looks like and how the lure got its name. To fish
the Booby successfully, use it with a very fast sinking line –
the Wet Cel Hi-D is one of the more popular – and a very
short cast, as little as nine inches in some cases. I now
prefer to use two Boobies, one five feet from the fly line,
the other about two feet from the first. You cast out the
lures and let the line sink down, keeping your eyes on the
nymphs until they disappear. It is then up to you to decide
when to start to retrieve, although the longer you wait the
deeper they will dive. As you start to retrieve, the by now
sunken line will pull the nymphs along the bottom where
their natural buoyancy will keep them from snagging. The
retrieve should then take them along the bottom where the
fish are feeding. As you start to lift your line the Boobies
will follow, but it is a good idea to pause in your retrieve
with about ten feet of fly-line left in the water. You'll be
surprised at how many takes you get at this point from fish
who have been following the nymphs to the surface and
assume they are either in trouble or getting ready to leave
the water.

Boobies come in all shapes, sizes and colours; the choice
is yours. They are best fished in a flat calm with the sun
shining and provide a good way of taking fish on a day
when most other methods may fail.

Scottish anglers have also been finding buzzers popular
and successful in taking rainbow trout. There are two
different methods. The first uses a floating line with a team
of buzzers tied on to the cast. The cast is then greased and
Fuller's earth is placed on the buzzers which will enable
you to hold them just under the surface at the point where
the trout can be seen taking. This can be particularly
effective for fishing down the wind slicks on the water,
those long calm patches or the dirty scum lanes that can be

created by a good hard blow. Fish can usually be seen moving in these lanes and nine times out of ten they will be feeding on trapped buzzers trying to break free of the surface film.

The other method of buzzer-fishing uses a dry buzzer, the Shipman's being the most popular. All you have to do is effectively reverse the previous procedure, with the cast degreased and floatant put on. Shipman buzzers are tied with a body of seal fur – or a substitute – which soak up the floatant and also provide a nice juicy target on the surface for the trout. You watch the direction in which your selected fish is moving then cast your buzzers into its path and leave them static. Then all you have to do is keep in touch with your cast of buzzers and wait for the fish to strike. If you are lucky enough to come across a shoal of rainbows using this method it is not uncommon to take two or even three trout at the same time. Bear in mind that it does take a little bit of practice to perfect this method – and one final piece of advice: don't strike!

Rainbows can also be caught with the Dry Fly using the same two techniques as I outlined for the buzzer, and again the static method seems to be most successful. The most popular colour appears to be ginger, with the best patterns the Soldier Palmer and the Wingless Wickham. Don't get me wrong, other anglers will prefer other patterns, but if you are trying this method for the first time you need look no further than these two.

Wet Fly fishing also accounts for many a good bag of rainbow trout these days with the favourite method being just as you would use for brown trout; a floating line or an Intermediate if conditions allow. This used to be my favourite method for fishing on the Lake of Menteith, as it was always very successful. Perhaps someday I may revert to it.

I will admit to enjoying fishing for rainbows; they seem to be less wary than browns except in shallow clear water where they can move just as quickly. I probably fish more

The grin says it all . . . a good fish on a self-tied fly

for them these days than brown trout although I still manage the odd visit to the many hill lochs in my area. Even then I occasionally return with a rainbow since so many of these hill lochs stock them to supplement their numbers, especially in the summer when the brownies tend to disappear in daylight. With escapees from fish farms, they can also be found along the west coast, swimming in the sea lochs and the rivers that feed into them. These rainbows are bars of silver and pound for pound fight as well as a sea trout. In fact, anglers unfamiliar with rainbows often mistake the two.

These fish farms have caused quite a lot of controversy, with various experts now linking them with the disappearance of sea trout stocks. I am sure it is one of the contributions, though I am also sure there is more to it. My other fear is that over-stocking of rainbows in brown trout waters will overturn the balance that should be maintained if the brown trout are to survive. An excellent example of this was at Loch Awe when a reported half million rainbows escaped into the loch. All sorts of rumours were being bandied about regarding this disaster. This number of fish released into a water 27 miles long need not have raised an eyebrow, especially when it did not take too long for the 'black bag brigade' to arrive on the scene and proceed to remove them by the bagful. All that was heard for a long time was that no browns were being caught, only rainbows. This was just not true, as anglers were indeed catching fair numbers of brown trout; those that fished for them that is. For a long time there were more concentrating on catching as many rainbows as possible thus neglecting the browns.

During those glorious days of the Awe rainbows there were some absolutely cracking fish coming off the Loch and for a short spell the British record was held with a fish of 20 lb plus. There were plenty of fish around the 5 to 6 lb mark being caught by all sort of methods and even now there are still rainbows being caught, although most of them are fairly small fish around the ½ lb mark. What I would like to know is, where are these small, good conditioned fish coming from. Are they breeding? This will no doubt be something to get our teeth into in the next few years, as more and more reports of small three inch fish are being reported all over Scotland.

For the 'any-method' angler you have the sea lochs that I have mentioned, also the rivers where it is permissible and some fisheries around the country also cater for those who wish to fish with bait. These are great for kids to help get them into fishing as there is every chance that they will catch something. There are several waters which even have special pools for the kids to enjoy themselves, and the odd adult can sometimes be found around the edges of the beginner's pools when the going gets tough in the fly only pools. Angling is a great sport in which to get children interested, as it is healthy and does a good job of keeping them off the streets and getting them into the country where they can also learn a lot about our countryside and the wildlife.

COARSE SCOTLAND

Jim Brown

With so much superb trout and salmon fishing, Scotland has never been known as a coarse-fishing area. Indeed, with perch and pike traditionally killed as vermin, you might think there would be no future for coarse anglers north of Carlisle. You could not, in fact, be further from the truth.

My first memories of coarse angling cover the period from the late '50s to the mid-'60s when my school friends and I would fish the Forth and Clyde Canal around Kirkintilloch. By today's standards our tackle was very basic; a spinning rod of around 7 feet, a fixed spool reel with 5 or 6 lb line, a cork for a float, a size 8 or 10 hook, and a bunch of worms or some flour and water paste.

We caught perch and pike in fairly large numbers along with a few roach and eels, which were frequently killed and fed to a local cat. Sadly, we knew no better and it would be some time before we learned the folly of our youthful ways. Our fishing was often interrupted by the boats from the fishing fleet which used the canal to pass from the west coast waters to the North Sea. On one memorable occasion we were even disturbed by a midget submarine.

In my later teens fishing took a back seat to wine, women and a lovely old Ford Anglia. Sense prevailed after a few years and the fishing bug returned. I had, however, no real urge to fish for trout or salmon – everyone else did that. I wanted to be different and, with sea fishing too far away, it had to be coarse.

Around this time I had started to notice busloads of anglers appearing on our canal most weekends between March and June. These were match anglers from the north of England who had come to fish our waters during their close season. The sight of anglers every 15 yards along the towpath with their long nets in the water was totally alien to me. They even returned their fish to the water when

A bonnie fish, the roach

they had been weighed at the end of their competitions. I had never seen anything like it.

Watching these men with their 2 lb lines and their tiny hooks and floats was a revelation to me. They spoke of wagglers, darts, swingtips, pinkies, squatts and casters. Absolutely marvellous, but what in heaven's name were all these things? Luckily there was a club in Glasgow to provide some of the answers. My home town of Kirkintilloch seemed to be a magnet for like-minded anglers because I found half a dozen living less than half a mile from me who were also members of the Glasgow club. It soon became clear that match fishing was our passion and we formed our own club, the Kirkintilloch Match Angling Club – better known then and now as K-MAC. We were not alone, however. Clubs were springing up throughout the central belt and it became clear that a national body was needed. This led to the formation of the SFCA, quickly recognised by the Sports Council as the governing body.

One of the most absorbing parts of our sport quickly became the discovery of new venues. The list grew rapidly. There was the canal, of course, Hogganfield Loch, the superb carp venue at Lanark Loch, our only bream venue at Lochmaben, Loch Ken near Castle Douglas, Loch Lomond, and the Tay at Perth – still the home of Scotland's finest roach. But it was the canal which took up most of our time because during the '70s it was full of roach, and Kelvinhead near Kilsyth was known far and wide for the quality and quantity of its fish.

Sadly, most of the roach were wiped out by disease in the late '70s and are only now returning to anything like their former levels. Fortunately, however, tench were establishing a foothold at the same time and spreading rapidly through most of the canal. Fish of over 5 lb are not uncommon and bags in excess of 70 lb have been recorded. Perch also suffered badly but they too are making a comeback. Only the pike has been ever-present, with fish of over 20 lb caught and returned each year.

This marvellous old waterway is once again a thriving fishery and haven for wildlife. You may even see the elusive kingfisher or, on a dawn session, perhaps the odd deer, even in built-up areas where they have followed the towpath. Prospects for the '90s are also looking good.

The Monklands Canal in Coatbridge is an excellent example of what can be done with co-operation between the local angling club and a district council. Together they have transformed a disused, overgrown and badly silted stretch of canal in Drumpellier Country Park into a fine fishery with over 100 pegs, well stocked with carp, roach, perch and bream. The carp were initially stocked at between 4 and 8 oz but can now be caught at over 2 lb. What better introduction to the sport for a youngster than to hook into one of these superb little fighters, while not too far away is another water with huge potential in Strathclyde Country Park. This loch is better known for its other water sports, but it contains roach and bream and as it matures and continues to receive more fish I am sure that it will become a venue of national and even international importance.

As our rivers and lochs become cleaner it is particularly heart-warming to see the improvement in the River Clyde. Although it has attracted publicity for the return of salmon and sea trout to the lower reaches below Motherwell, there has also been a population explosion of dace, roach and other coarse fish. The stretch from Blantyre to Cambuslang is well worth a visit, with nets of up to 20 lb of dace and roach quite possible. From Dalmarnock down to Glasgow Green, however, the river is controlled by tidal sluice gates and is very deep with strong undercurrents. You can find 20 feet of water only a few feet from the bank so you must never attempt to wade in these lower reaches – even though, with care, match catches to 28 lb have been recorded. Glasgow can take pride in a river in which it is possible to catch a net full of fish only a mile from town.

Now we no longer have to stay in the central belt for our fishing, though. South-west Scotland is brimming with coarse fish in the man-made fisheries springing up with increasing regularity and in many of the major lochs in the area. You could spend a full year down here and not cover them all.

Along with the increase in popularity, however, the past ten years have also brought many improvements in tackle, with rods much lighter now and reels much harder wearing. You can see poles of up to 15 metres in length – unheard of even five years ago – and they are now even lighter than ever. I also welcome the fact that we are using non-toxic weights and that anglers are becoming more and more the watchdogs of our rivers and lochs. We are often the first to notice when pollution or other problems appear and we can help to keep our waterways healthy.

It is now not uncommon for match fishing competitions to attract more than 100 competitors and our premier event, the Summer League, now has more than 20 teams competing, with many of them sponsored by a local shop or a major manufacturer. The top men each year are eligible for selection to the international team and I hope that one day Scotland will host the World Championships. What a boost that would be, but there is much work to be done before we realise that particular dream.

THE LIGHTER SIDE OF HEAVYWEIGHT

Stan Massey

The weights being recorded, compared to those of years now long gone, could best be described as sad.

'Nice cod, mate! Three pound five ounces. You'll be buying the drinks tonight.' 'Forget it,' another steward chipped in, 'the guy over there's got a 5-pounder.'

I was surrounded by at least another 400 anglers all eagerly watching the weigh-in at one of Scotland's top shore angling competitions. The '5-pounder' did indeed put its captor in line to buy the drinks. No other cod had come close. In spite of the fact that close to a thousand, well experienced anglers had travelled to the Clyde Estuary to take part in the event, less than 30 cod had been landed and this from an area that had once been described as the 'sea angling Mecca of Europe'. As well as being Scotland's largest shore competition, this event was also one of the longest running.

I had faithfully attended every November for at least 15 years and had watched the bags drop from weights of 40 lb, 50 lb and in one year over 90 lb per rod to single figures. Commercial operations (and, it must be said, greedy, profit-orientated anglers) had raped the Clyde grounds. Areas which were once the spawning grounds of massive shoals of Atlantic cod were now all but devoid of the species. A

Robert Richardson with the new Scottish and IGFA 50 lb line class world record porbeagle shark of 414 lb

few showed up each year but in fractions of a per cent of the quantities we had known in the '60s and '70s.

As I drove home to Glasgow that wet November evening in 1989, I reflected on the decline in fishing around Scotland, but more importantly I considered the anglers involved, myself included. It seemed as though we were happy to accept the situation and to plod on in an apathetic manner in the hope of the odd fish. The gear we used – in fact, the gear readily available to us from the angling retailers – was primitive compared to the south of England, and, in comparison with charter boats in, say Devon and Cornwall, the boats we hired were little better than dug-out canoes. Scottish sea angling had slipped into the doldrums and it was high time something was done about it.

I have never been one to sneak away from a challenge and the revitalising of Scottish sea angling would indeed be a daunting one. I was one individual with an idea in my head. There was no way that I could ever hope to alter the general angling scene but what if I could introduce a brand new branch to it?

Having suffered from 'anglingitis' for over 30 years, I had long been discarded by friends (the few I had left) and relatives alike as a hopeless case. Years ago I had given up hope of finding a discreet advert in the press: 'Do you have an angling problem? Do you need help? Phone . . .' and Anglers Anonymous had not yet been invented – although a few wives had no doubt tried. I had to have my weekly injection of 'line wetting' or suffer the indignity of sweats and shakes. A hopeless case, indeed!

We all know what is said about 'clouds and silver linings' and even my peculiar – although not unique – disease had one. Thinking it over, I slowly came to realise that what I had lost out on over the years in the way of parties, dances and general high living had been replaced by not a little experience and knowledge about fish and fishing. The many, many long, cold and usually fishless nights of anti-social (almost weird) behaviour on numerous wind-swept piers and rock gullies or on the deck of some heaving, foul-smelling *African Queen* had at very least given me the opportunity to try most aspects of angling, and perhaps that hard-earned information could be of use now.

I had fished for most species in British waters from the lordly salmon to the humble mackerel. I enjoyed the sport offered by all of them but my first love had to be what is generally called 'deep sea' angling. Why it was given such a name I have yet to find out. Most of it is carried out in relatively shallow waters close to shore. However, amongst the vast array of species I had caught – or, in many cases, 'blanked' on – was the emotive sounding shark. They rank amongst the minority on my species list as I had actually caught them, mostly on holiday trips in the south of England. I had a good knowledge of the techniques used for sharking and the idea began to take shape that, given a few more lunatics like myself, we may just be able to put together a group to go look for these beasties with teeth.

Over the next few evenings I imitated a monk as I pondered the possibilities. Eventually, she who can do no wrong was prompted to ask if I was ill, dying or merely going into one of my regular anti-social moods. A few minutes more deep thought brought the revelation: 'I'm going to start a club to catch sharks in Scotland.'

'Oh yes,' says she, continuing ironing, 'that will be nice.'

I had been warned that years of angling and its eccentricities tends to immunise one's partner to such a point that absolutely nothing relating to the sport affects them. (That's not quite true. She was strangely affected one evening the previous year when, having returned home earlier than expected, she found me diligently pulping frozen worm and crab in the liquidiser. No sense of humour, women!).

I had always been a bit of a loner when it came to angling, a member of a few clubs over the years but much preferring to experiment on unusual species and techniques rather than running with the crowd. This left me with a void as to how a club should be formed and operated.

'Who cares. Let's just do it anyway and worry about the organisation later.'

I spent long evenings poring over old reports, books, commercial publications and the like gleaning every and all information on large, unusual fish around Scotland. Basically, the club would be formed to explore and develop fishing for such species. All of them were heavyweights and, in an attempt to isolate them from the run-of-the-mill fish most anglers go after, I decided on species capable of attaining at least 75 lb in weight – affording the club with a variety of targets such as blue, porbeagle and thresher shark, tope, common skate, halibut, and conger eel. (When the 75 lb figure was later accepted at our inaugural meeting, it formed the basis of the criteria of 'big-game' species for club purposes and as such encompassed cod and ling, both of which have attained more than 75 lb when commercially caught.)

Information on times and areas where we could contact such fish was not too difficult to obtain. Conger eel were normally caught by accident in Scotland, although a few dedicated anglers fished for them on purpose. They are fairly widespread on rough ground and wrecks, although with a Scottish record of 48 lb at that time – it is now over 60 lb – Scottish eels fell far short of the 90 and 100 lb specimens caught on a regular basis in England.

Skate fishing in Scotland was already legendary, with massive common skate, upwards of 200 lb, having been taken in Orkney, Shetland, Ullapool and, of course, the famous grounds off the Isle of Mull. Although such fish were well known, it was still only small specialist groups who tried for them. Indeed, many travelled from the continent to fish the Scottish grounds, such was the reputation. These fish we would look at closely as the seasons progressed in the hope of finding even more untried grounds, which I knew existed.

Tope, a true member of the shark family, were caught on the west and south-west coasts of Scotland every summer from around June to October. I had landed many of these fine sporting fish over the years and I knew they would be a good introduction to big-game angling should we recruit 'novice' anglers to the club. They can run to about the 80 lb mark, although I am fairly certain that tope of around 100 lb will exist somewhere. When fished for on light tackle with lines of 12–20 lb breaking-strains, they offer excellent fun and are a comparatively easy crack at a big fish for anglers more used to 5–15 lb pollack and cod.

The far north of Scotland and, in particular, the Pentland Firth grounds and seas around Orkney and Shetland are home to the largest flatfish in the world, the giant halibut. Non-anglers see halibut in the fishmongers and, as some have told me, assume it to be a normal flatfish of, say, 5 lb. Nothing could be further from the truth. Halibut is a fierce predator reaching many hundreds of pounds in weight. They have been recorded upwards of 500 lb by commercial boats and many believe they may reach up to 800 to 1,000 lb and lengths of ten or so feet. The British record rod-caught fish of over 200 lb comes from these grounds in the north of Scotland but, as we were later to find out, the seas in these areas can be none too friendly either to anglers or commercial operators – possibly one reason why few halibut are taken on rod and line.

Shark! A species anglers and non-anglers all know and can readily identify. It was surprising to me, however, just how few people realise that large shark swim in Scottish waters, often extremely close to shore. Hundreds of porbeagles are landed commercially every year around the coast and these can be enormous. I was once given a photo of a huge 31-stone (438 lb) porbeagle which was taken in the Forth Estuary by a commercial boat – a fish over 8½ feet in length. Indeed, many porbeagle in the 200–300 lb range are taken each year but a more average weight would be about 120–200 lb.

Porbeagle are not the only large sharks evident around
Scotland. Thresher, possibly the most readily identifiable
species because of their hugely elongated upper tail lobe,
have been seen in the Minch, outer Clyde, Loch Fyne,
Arran, Mull of Galloway and Luce Bay areas, although
none have, as yet, been landed on rod and line here. They
have been hooked by anglers fishing other species though.
Similarly, the blue shark is known to hunt in packs and
have been taken, again commercially, from a variety of
venues in Scotland. A few have been taken on rod and line,
but few serious attempts have been made on them.

The mako shark, possibly the most dangerous variety as
far as anglers are concerned, have been taken in nets
around the south-west of Scotland and have also been
identified by divers off the Western Isles, although how
accurate these reports may be is unknown. They are probably the fastest shark in the world, renowned for leaping,
sometimes as high as 20 feet or more, but the sad fact
is that on a number of occasions mako have actually leapt
into a boat and caused serious damage and injury. I have
had no personal exprience – thank goodness – of eye-
balling one underwater but I can imagine that it would be
difficult to differentiate between a mako and porbeagle
unless you had witnessed such fish on many occasions.
Mako, porbeagle and great white shark are the three
members of the mackerel shark family, and although the
size differential can be vast, with whites reaching upwards
of 5,000 lb, identification could be a problem in murky
waters and given only a quick glance of the fish.

Other cold water sharks such as the six-gilled and the
greenland all exist around Scotland, although an encounter
with them at this stage would more than likely be by luck –
good or bad has yet to be seen!

Having armed myself with a variety of information on
the species we would be searching for, I placed a few
adverts in the angling and local press as well as tackle
and sports shops. I had hoped for half a dozen or so to join

me and was pleasantly surprised when, at the inaugural meeting in 1990, 16 anglers attended. Of these founder members, only a handful other than myself had fished for heavyweights in the past. Nevertheless we were fortunate at that meeting to have two or three members of the Mull of Galloway Big Game Club attend. This club, although little has been heard of it in recent years, had worked hard locating shark and other heavyweights in the '60s and '70s.

The usual formalities were thrashed out, a constitution was drafted and International Game Fish Association Rules were adopted. The Big-Game Club of Scotland was decided on as a name and it looked to me as if all would be plain sailing. How wrong I was to be.

Prior to the meeting, and being an eternal optimist, I had undertaken to book about 15 charters, mostly in the Mull of Galloway area and mostly for sharking. These were quickly filled by budding Zane Greys and I soon had to book many more. We spread these around the country, from the Mull of Galloway, to Skye and to the Pentland Firth. In fact, by the end of that season we had booked 62 charters. These filled fairly easily, simply because of continued publicity and the fact that we attracted some 50 members in our first year.

Even with 50 members, though, we still had only six or seven who had tried big-game fishing in the past, and they spent a lot of time trying to explain tackle and techniques to the 'novices'. I emphasise the word novice because most of the members were perfectly competent and experienced anglers in their own right; they were just new to big-game angling.

The first shark charter arrived in April of that year and half-a-dozen members duly appeared on the quay armed with a variety of tackle that had been purchased as suitable for the job. I myself operate a small business hand-crafting big-game fishing-rods and have done so for close on 20 years. I looked at some of the gear that was being stowed on board and experienced my first twinge of doubt. This

Stan Massey. Pork pie or Rubby Dubby for lunch? (Dubby tasted better!)

wasn't going to be as easy as I had thought.

Sport-fishing or big-game fishing has a world governing body, the IGFA, mentioned earlier. Without becoming too technical, I would have to explain that this body sets out line classes of 2, 4, 8, 12, 16, 20, 30, 50, 80 and 130 lb breaking-strain line. The IGFA maintain world records for hundreds of species of fish caught on lines within the various categories. The home of sport-fishing (and, indeed, the IGFA) is on the Florida coast. This is also the area where perhaps the majority of quality sport-fishing tackle originates but not all of it. What does originate there is a good working standard, though.

There are hundreds, if not thousands, of items of fishing tackle available but the most obvious, other than the hook, is the rod, reel and line. I surveyed the collection of rods and reels being loaded on to the boat that morning in dismay. Most were British-made and I do not feel it necessary to apologise to the major manufacturers of UK tackle when I say most of the items they sell as being 'big-game' tackle is nonsense, the rods in particular. The IGFA line classes afford a standard for 'balanced tackle' – that is tackle designed to operate effectively with that test of line. For most British sharking, I had advised the members to buy 30 lb or 50 lb equipment – 30 lb being ample but 50 lb better for the novice. The guys had listened and bought just that: some had even bought 80 lb class. The problem was that their rods were all 'off the shelf' UK rods and even the 80 lb rods were at best 30 lb class when compared with Florida standards. I could see I was going to have to explain every aspect in detail, especially the fact that 'true' IGFA equipment is extremely powerful when compared to British equipment. Most British 50 lb rods are comparable to a 12 lb or 16 lb Florida rod and obviously hopeless for landing heavy fish such as shark on a regular basis.

My next surprise was in the concoction of 'additives' that had been brought along to brew up that strange British item of shark angling known affectionately as 'rubby-dubby'. Other countries call it 'chum' or 'berely', (pronounced 'burly'), but for reasons known only to the British we call it rubby-dubby. However, as British shark angling really developed in the Cornwall and Devon areas, I have a sneaking suspicion that the term originated in some dark Cornish tavern after an excess of scrumpy. I also believe that the name, and indeed the whole concept of dubby, is a ploy of the Cornish Republican Army to do away with the rest of the UK population on the quiet – anglers first.

And what exactly is this strange item? Those of you who are familiar with *Macbeth* will remember the witches brewing concoctions in their cauldrons. Well, dubby is possibly best likened to this, although much more potent. At its most basic, it is a mixture of minced or chopped fish, preferably oily, such as herring, pilchard or mackerel, and preferably a bit on the smelly side. So the concoctions of rotten cod heads, whiting backbone, squid tentacles and (although I still find it hard to believe) chicken giblets, heads and feet which appeared on the quay that dismal morning had to be smelled to be believed. The dismembered chickens had been obtained from a well-meaning butcher 11 days previously and had been kept in a plastic bag in a garage. I was also informed by the proud owner of this chemical reaction that the whiting remains had been acquired three days prior to the chicken and stored in the same bag. I looked at the rubber gloves I carried for mixing dubby and wondered about their resistance to acids and corrosives.

The normal method of utilising this mixture would be to bulk it up with bran and oil and hang it over the boat side in onion-bags so that it slowly filtered out creating a slick of fishy smelling particles which attracts the shark to the boat.

Exactly what could be done with this mixture I did not know. If we were to put it in the sea, would we be liable to charges of some sort for pollution? Would Greenpeace picket our next charter? Oh well, we had to make the best of it.

The next chapter in that first day's episode was the look of abject horror on the face of the 'skipper'. I emphasise the word since we were to find out after a good few abortive trips with this particular man that his knowledge of shark angling, possibly angling in general, was on a par with my own personal knowledge of nuclear physics. This look of horror was his reaction to the dubby. We were later to find out that certain items of tackle were frowned upon on his boat which was his pride and joy – items such as rods, reels, line, hooks, bait etc. etc. In fact, anything at all which could make the boat dirty. I assume he was more used to anglers from the stockbroker belt who turned up in pin-stripes. Anyway, he must be a decent chap since he always passes his clients on to other skippers after the first trip.

Needless to say, we really emphasised the club's policy of 'conservation by example' on that trip. We didn't harm a single shark.

The experience of the dubby on that trip seemed to me to have approached the ultimate in human degradation but later that year I was to become involved with one trip where the dubby was almost beyond the bounds of the English language to describe. A certain skipper who goes by the name of Gordon Stewart (I don't mind naming him as he is a good friend and first-class skipper) who operates out of Scrabster in Caithness, had prepared well for the club trip for shark by gathering plenty of oily fish in a large dustbin which was stored on the boat. Once we had reached the grounds that day he told me of the dubby in the bin and I started to scoop into it ready for a day's sharking. What he had not told me was that his bin had been filled in preparation for our trip *seven weeks* earlier and had been left on the boat, in summer, for the whole time. As the scoop broke the surface film, I experienced a strange sensation at my nostrils. They suddenly felt warm and sticky. My head also felt a bit strange. Whatever the dubby had become – it was now obvious some chemical change had taken place – the fumes from it had burst the blood vessels in my nose and I was bleeding profusely . . . to the accompaniment of the crew – and skipper – throwing up, first in stereo and then in quadraphonic.

Never before, and I hope never in the future, had we smelled anything remotely like this mixture. Sea birds in the area took off for pastures green and even the seals vanished. The smell did not give up and we considered that there was a very real danger that the adhesives holding the wooden boat hull would give. The bin had to go. Votes were taken and, as always, I was the lucky one. The skipper had no say in the matter. He was the obvious culprit and was nominated by all. To much retching and soul searching, the offending article was deposited into the Pentland Firth and sank with gas bubbles and froth creating a maelstrom around the boat. Such are the joys of rubby dubby.

The season progressed and more and more of the novices gained experience. We found sources for more suitable big-game tackle and things began to look good. As I had believed, the Tope trips were popular with Mike Watson, a skipper from Stranraer, finding us good grounds where we took fish up to the 50 lb mark. All the guys enjoyed these trips. Some of them were wary at first when I suggested they fish for Tope on a maximum of 20-class gear but, as they realised just how powerful a 20-class IGFA outfit was, the doubts vanished and they enjoyed the Tope fishing on light gear.

Conger trips were organised and a few of the members who had tried for conger in the past found success. None of the fish were large by English standards but the members enjoyed organised excursions for these large eels rather than taking them by chance. The best for the season was a 44 lb eel by Kenny Leonard which, although not huge, was only 4 lb under the Scottish record at that time.

Shark were still proving elusive but we continued trying until some bright spark suggested we try mixing blood with the dubby. Copious amounts were obtained from a friendly slaughter-house – an abattoir which slaughtered fish of course, because mammalian blood is illegal under IGFA rules. Vast quantities of red and white corpuscles were dumped into various sections of sea along with a now much-refined mixture of dubby. Still no shark. On one occasion in the Cromarty Firth area there was a slight error of judgment when the wrong tap on the blood container was opened. The entire area around the boat turned red to the extent that we kept a look out for Sea King helicopters of Search and Rescue in the belief that they would assume a 747 jet had crashed into the water. The blood practice was considered a waste of time and we reverted to normal(?) dubby.

Around that period we were contacted by members of the Sportfishing Club of the British Isles, in particular Dave Sneath and Vic Sampson. Dave is the publicity officer and Vic is probably Britain's most famous shark angler having a good number of great whites to his credit including one of 1,704 lb in 1991 which is the largest taken on rod and line, worldwide, for about 30 years. The SCBI members offered us a lot of advice and assistance and our two clubs have an excellent working relationship, with possibly the largest collection of big-game fishing knowledge in the UK between us.

As is always the case with clubs, you have a nucleus of die-hards while the remainder of the membership is keen enough to try a few trips each year and just keep in touch. We were no exception. Various discussions were held between the regulars and we decided that the extreme north of Scotland was possibly our best chance of a shark as there had been numerous reports of anglers sighting porbeagle and also losing other species of fish to them. The only minor drawback was that this always seemed to take place around January and February.

If you are unfamiliar with Caithness and the Pentland Firth, then I could best describe it as rugged and desolate.

The waters of the Pentland are notorious and the tide-rips awesome but this is the type of ground porbeagle like. Now few sane people would leave a warm fire in February to travel 300 miles to the extreme north of Scotland, board a boat in, shall we say, none too calm weather, to go fishing for a species more normally associated with warm climates and tropical seas. Anglers, of course, are not renowned for sanity.

Trips were booked with Claire Calder, another fine skipper, and Gordon Stewart. The week before we were due to travel I had a phone call from Dave Proudfoot, Secretary of the Caithness Sea Angling Club. He had just hooked and landed a 198 lb porbeagle from Claire's boat, and congratulations were duly dished out – along with other mutterings not heard on the phone. At least it seemed as though the theory was going to prove correct.

Two members, Murdo Gunn and Bill Hutchison – both black belts in insanity – battled through snow-storms and conditions more reminiscent of the Glasgow Fair to meet Claire at Scrabster. Weather was none too hospitable but the dynamic duo decided, 'To hell with it, we're going out.' On arrival at the chosen shark grounds about 30 minutes' steam from Scrabster, hopes were raised when a shark was seen at the surface. Baitfish were quickly landed and 50-class shark gear free-lined over the side using 1–2 lb coalfish as bait. The waiting was kept to a minimum as Murdo bent into the first shark. The fish sounded deep and Murdo dug in his heels and started to pump – that is, lift and lower the rod tip, with the line wound on to the reel on the downstroke. If nothing else we're innovative in Scotland, and since the guys weren't on a Florida game boat with a fighting chair, they improvised. A chair was made up using buckets and fish-boxes and just over an hour later a 160 lb porbeagle was on the boat.

Bill got his chance as well that day when he boated an even bigger fish of just under 190 lb. The determination had paid off at the most unlikely time of the year. A few weeks later on the same boat, another of the members, Joe Connolly, lost a fish of about 170 lb after a battle lasting almost an hour. Just as we thought it was beat and Dave Proudfoot and myself were about to grab the trace, the fish made a last dive and cut the line on the hull. Dave, who lives in the area and has much more chance than us to fish it, landed a huge porbeagle of 350 lb a few weeks later. Needless to say, the Scrabster trips in February are well booked up for the next few seasons much to the displeasure of other clubs, I'm told.

We tried a variety of venues in our first season and came into contact with some real characters. I'm still trying to fathom some of them out. We have a real gentleman of a member who really could do no wrong in this world. Nothing is too much trouble and he is always eager to try new ideas, but he is also an enigma. He is almost fanatical on wildlife conservation and saving the seals and whales, but his great ambition is to stick a large lump of metal into the mouth of a shark and haul it into a boat.

Big-game fishing in Scotland is in its infancy but given a few seasons we have the potential to develop a sport-fishery on a par with some of the best anywhere. We have the species already mentioned and we are looking closely at the possibilities of big-eye and bluefin tuna. Broadbill swordfish and white and mako sharks are also a possibility. Should we discover any of these world-class game fish, we have the experience of the SCBI membership to call on if needed. We have also managed to get involved with tagging research in conjunction with Glasgow Museum's Natural History Department. Such a project can only assist our own research and help to ensure that stocks are not wiped out by mass slaughter as happened in the English Channel area.

The efforts of the club members were finally justified when, in March 1992, Robert Richardson landed a new Scottish and IGFA world record porbeagle shark, weighing 414 lb, 200 yards offshore from a mark near Scrabster.

SHORE,
TO BE SURE

Hugh Smith

Like so many others, my first taste of fishing came on the Clyde, Dunoon Pier to be exact, where I remember fishing with a hand line with my dad when I was about four or five. Sadly, my father died the following year and my fishing was limited to whenever my mother could manage the odd day trip to Saltcoats.

However, it was when I was about 12 that I got hooked in a big way. By this time I had graduated to day trips fishing off Craigendoran Pier. We had friends who lived in an old railway cottage which was practically on the sea front and after one particularly hard day's fishing off the pier and in the sea they asked me to stay overnight. That overnight stay turned into a six week summer holiday and every glorious day was spent fishing with the local lads. When I got home I saved all my pocket money until I had raised the princely sum of 10/6d (52½p) to buy the type of light spinning-rod I had been fishing with all summer. My grandad came to the rescue with a reel to go with it; an Intrepid Monarch with a bail arm which hit the stem of the handle and engaged the line. The fun I had catching codling, mackerel and flounders, all of which bent the rod double!

By this time I had persuaded some friends to come with me to Craigendoran every week. It started with two or three of us but eventually there were 14 of us at a time. But at the age of 14 I was ready to set my sights further afield and over the sea to Gourock. None of my pals would go with me but I was undaunted and after a long bus journey I finally found myself on Gourock Pier, which to my amazement was lined along its whole length with people fishing. When I inquired what you caught there a man asked me for my name, put it on a piece of paper, and demanded half a crown (12½p). I quickly pointed out that you can fish Craigendoran Pier for nothing and he just as quickly pointed out that he was Alister Forrest, he ran the Firth of Clyde Sea Anglers Association, and today he was organising an open competition.

I thought half a crown was a lot of money, especially when I checked my pockets to find I had only 1/10d (9p).

Shore fishing. South African style

Fortunately, Alister said he would make up the difference and I could fish with him; little did I know what this strange encounter would lead to ten years hence. I fished with Alister all day and while he took five codling I had one which weighed in at 1 lb 10 oz 11 dr – they were an organised club and I had a good set of scales. I was as surprised as anyone when my name was called out at the weigh-in as the winner of the junior section. That earned me my first trophy, a silver-plated double marmalade dish, and I was thrilled. Names and addresses were swapped, my pals and I joined the club the following week and I fished for the club for over 20 years as it went from strength to strength winning honours all over the country.

As the years went on I earned my first international cap and along with it the unforgettable feeling of fishing for your country. It's impossible to explain unless you've done it yourself, but I can assure you I was shaking from head to toe. Since then I have represented Scotland more than 60 times in Belgium, Portugal, France, Ireland, South Africa, and Kenya, meeting lots of anglers who are now friends and that's really what it's all about.

However, my greatest feeling of achievement came in 1976 when, along with Eddie Wason, John Hood, and Jimmy Miller – with Douglas Dallas as team manager – I represented Scotland in four Tests against South Africa. England, Germany and Belgium were also taking part.

The first test was in Durban. It was dark when we arrived but you could hear the awesome pounding of the Indian Ocean surf from our beachfront hotel. After breakfast we had our first practice match fishing in the South African style with the reel six inches from the bottom of the rod and the rod held in a holder on a belt round the waist. After two hours we had some small fish but nothing big and when we got back into the jeep we could feel that one side of our body was tingling. We had been sunburned down one side and were all two-toned, white and red. We didn't think the sun would be so hot before eight in the morning, but we learned our lesson and went out in the afternoon to do the other side.

On the day of the match the fishing was very poor but we learned that John had taken a 15 lb sand shark – a fish with the head of a ray and the body of a shark. There were a lot of small barbel which were not counted, though a spike in the hand from one of them would have meant a stay in hospital. John had also taken a ray and my own contribution amounted to being stripped twice to the bottom of my line by sharks which were just too big to be landed. But at the weigh in, to everyone's astonishment, Scotland had won the day. It was apparently the first time South Africa had ever been beaten at International level and there was much promising that it would also be the last.

The second day of the competition was much duller with a wind. The home side started well and landed two sharks of 100 lb within the first two hours. Jimmy hooked into a fish an hour into the match and had it on an hour later. I can still see him being pulled into the water, only held back by two burly South Africans in case the sharks decided to take Jim for a swim. By that point, however, all we had to show for our efforts were hard-luck stories. We had all hooked and lost big fish.

It may seem hard to believe that you can be dragged into the water by a big fish but it really does happen. You are standing there with your rod up straight in its holder when it is suddenly pulled down to the horizontal and line starts ripping off your reel at an alarming rate. You tighten your line and strike into the shark but the line is still tearing off. By now you don't know whether to apply more strain or keep it going, although after letting the first couple run and losing them, you soon learn you have to apply a good bit of pressure. Even so, the power of these fish is breathtaking and the line keeps going. By this time the South African guides who have been supplied two to a team are there to give you a hand because, with no line left, you will simply be dragged further and further down the beach.

The Scottish team did well!

I was sitting with my feet digging into the sand and behind, you could see the ploughed wake of where I had been. By this time all three of us were in the water up to our waists. One of the guides turned to the other and by the look on their faces I knew we had no chance of pulling this one in – it must have been a java or a large sand shark. Sadly, we had no option but to pull for a break and allow the line to part.

This happened three times that day and twice the day before. All I had to show for two days' fishing in Durban was lots of barbel, which were not allowed to be weighed in and a shad which was about 3 lb – or would have been had it not been chopped in half by a shark when I was reeling it in. The shark went for it about five yards away from where I had been wading earlier. Needless to say, I resolved there and then not to do any more wading.

But Jimmy had landed a 130 lb sand shark which eventually turned out to be the biggest fish of the entire trip. It had taken him two hours to land. I could see him from where I was fishing as he was pulled down into the water several times, only to walk back up the beach gaining line before running down to the water's edge retrieving as he went. Finally there was a massive commotion and a surge of white foam as four guides pulled this huge fish on to the beach by hand and the rest of the Scottish team were jumping for joy. At the weigh-in we had again won the day and had beaten the rest of the teams, including the South Africans, to take the gold medal.

But for all of these foreign adventures, I still love shore fishing in Scotland. It is my favourite type of angling, I think, because of its sense of independence; you simply go where you want and fish how you want. With a few exceptions, there are no permits or closed seasons like fresh-water anglers have. And unlike those who fish from boats, there are no arguments about which marks you should fish from. The shore angler is his own boss and, if he makes a mistake going to a mark which doesn't produce fish, then he has no one to blame but himself.

Bait is by far the most important part of fishing and if you don't spend a lot of time and effort at this stage you leave yourself at a big disadvantage. It doesn't matter if you have the best tackle money can buy or can cast farther than anyone else; you cannot catch fish on bare hooks. For me, bait collection starts at the end of a day's fishing. However, there are a great many anglers who don't know how to keep bait alive for a few days never mind a few months.

One of the best and most sought-after baits is peeler crab. Most anglers have their own favourite little beaches which they will search each week. Like me, they guard their secrets jealously, but don't be discouraged because I can assure you that most of the shore-line around our coast produces peeler crab. The first thing to look for are rocks or weeds or old cans – in fact, anything a crab can crawl into. If you look at the edges of these places you will usually see a small raised pile of sand and behind it, at the very back, occasionally a peeler crab. The crab will have dug out the sand and burrowed itself in for protection, but beware of the claws which can still inflict a nasty nip. If you do find a crab, you have to check that it is the right type – hard backs are no use for our kind of fishing – so to find out if it is a peeler simply turn the crab on its back and remove the tip of one of its middle legs by bending it back and forward and from side to side. If it is a peeler, the outside shell will crack leaving a soft replica underneath; a hardback will break off completely. Some anglers remove the whole leg but the tip is sufficient, and remember not to remove the back legs which the crab uses for swimming. If it is not a peeler it should be returned to its hideaway, and since the crab can regenerate lost limbs it should feel none the worse for its experience.

Please also remember that if you lift rocks with weeds attached then put them back exactly the way you got them to allow the beach to go on doing its job. If you just turn the rocks over and leave them they will lie on other weedy rocks which will not only kill the weeds but produce a foul smell. But more important than the weeds are the other life-forms which shelter under the rocks. Sea anemones, shrimps and other crustaceans will dry up very quickly if exposed to the sun, especially in summer. You'll be doing yourself a favour because, if you look after your beach, your beach will look after you by providing all the bait you need.

Rag worm is another popular bait and although digging for them is getting harder there are still some very good areas, especially on spring tides or when the moon is full and tides are lowest. The best type of ground is usually found around river mouths, harbours and mussel beds. My own method for checking on prospective ragworm areas is to walk along the shore and slowly press down hard with my foot. If I have chosen the right spot, then lots of small holes will appear and then disappear as the pressure forces water out of the worm holes.

Lug worms come from a slightly different type of ground and are very easy to find on sandy beaches. You can usually see the worm casts with air holes about eight inches away. If you draw an imaginary straight line between them and put your fork in about four inches either side of it you should find the worm as it burrows between the two points. I prefer the smaller black lugs which are tougher, stay on the hook better and live longer in the fridge. You can get rag worm amongst the lug but not the other way round since the rag are carnivorous and attack the other types, as I have found to my cost in the past. If you want to keep bait for a long time you must look after it as soon as you collect it. For worms, it is important to keep a bucket of fresh salt water handy to allow the worms to clean themselves out by passing the water through them and removing the excess sand. I usually change the water several times before heading home and if you do this you will see that each time there is less and less sand at the bottom of the bucket. But remember not to overcrowd them. Once home, the bait will have to be checked and separated, with the damaged worms removed into a separate container so they can be used first. Lug worms are not as hardy as rag and will need a bit more attention.

The ideal situation is to have a separate bait fridge, if only to prevent embarrassment when unsuspecting visitors pop into the kitchen for a snack. I think a second fridge is essential and worth its weight in gold to a sea angler, and once you have it set up with all your various containers, the next thing you want is an air pump which is the other important factor in keeping the bait fresh. My pump is on the outside of the fridge, with the air hose going through into the different bait trays. Whole worms last longer and are less work to keep alive after the first few days. Rag can last three to four weeks but they must be kept aerated.

White rag don't need aeration – in fact, I think they last longer without it, providing there are no more than ten or 12 to each tub. Whites can last for four or five months this way but the water must be changed regularly for the first week. There's no need to change the water too much after this unless it becomes discoloured, but always remember to use only sea water at the same temperature as the bait.

Keeping crab is relatively easy. Simply separate them into boxes on the basis of how soon they are likely to peel. Tomato boxes are perfect. I line the bottom with damp newspaper and put in some weed, not too much, and simply allow the crab to work its way down to its own level. Cover the box with two polythene bags – one from each end – which will not only help keep the crabs in but keep them moist by gathering condensation. Then you simply pop them into the fridge and check them every two days if possible.

So, given that the bait is fresh, you have picked the right place to go and most importantly that the fish are co-operative, you can look forward to a wonderful day's sport . . . although I would like to see more control over our commercial fishing fleet.

We lost the three-mile limit several years ago which allowed bigger boats into the Clyde. That did a lot of damage, but we all managed to get our share of fish though when they got scarce the trawlers turned to the prawns. They scraped the bottom and scooped everything into their small nets. The immature fish didn't stand a chance, ended up floating on the surface and the gulls had a field day. In the last five years, I feel the prawn trawlers have done a great deal more damage to the sea bed and reduced recruitment of fish stocks than all the legal and illegal trawling done before the three-mile limit was lifted.

The Cod wars with Iceland proved you can regenerate fish stocks. Iceland has a fishing limit inside which no foreign trawlers are allowed. They also have a seven-mile limit used as a nursery. Only commercial long-line fishermen and anglers are allowed to fish this area. It has made a fantastic difference and when I was there in 1986, the fishing was great. We had cod to 20 lb, haddock to 10 lb, with halibut and many other species. The fishing in Iceland is now the envy of Europe and we should learn before it is too late.

Scotland has so much to offer with its wonderfully rugged coastline and when the sun is in the sky, the surf is rolling in and the fish are in the mood, there is nowhere else in the world I would rather be, to be shore!

A FITTY PEAK

Gerald MacKenzie

Reservoirs and dams often make good trout fisheries, but there is no doubt that a natural loch makes the best trout fishery of them all. Trout have happily made their home in countless lochs all over Scotland and now comfortably share some of the lowland lochs with their American cousin, the rainbow trout.

Loch Fitty is one such water, a mixed rainbow and brown trout fishery lying approximately three miles north-east of Dunfermline in the ancient Scottish Kingdom of Fife. It is a shallow loch, made during the last ice age when an enormous piece of ice settled on the land and compressed it to form an inland water. Over the last hundred years, though, West Fife coal mining operations altered a small part of the shoreline but with the mines now long since closed, it takes a keen eye to see where the land was disturbed.

The waters which supply Loch Fitty rise from the western edge of the Cleish Hills. Much of the underlying rock there is limestone, giving the water a pH higher than 7, with that extra sparkle of an alkaline loch and encouraging an abundance of fauna in the shape of fresh-water shrimp, water slater, the common wandering snail and Jenkins' spire shell snail, all of which thrive in the loch and on which the trout eagerly feed. Indeed, the spire shell – so popular as a food with the rainbow trout – has an interesting tale. The story goes that it came into this country on the bottom of wooden sailing boats trading with the Dutch East Indies and, in the mid- to late 1800s, settled in the brackish waters of the Thames estuary. Since that time this small creature – only 4–5 mm tall – has spread all over the country and is very common wherever it is found. It reproduces without the male sex and, like freshwater winkles, does not lay eggs, but gives birth to living young.

Runrig drummer Ian Bayne with Loch Fitty rainbows

The native brown trout (*Salmo trutta*) is protected by law and anglers may not fish them between 7 October and 14 March when they are spawning and therefore replenishing the stock for the seasons to come. Rainbow trout (*Salmo gairdneri*, more recently *Oncorhyncus mykiss*), however, not being indigenous to the British Isles, do not have a close season by law, although some water authorities in England have a close season which includes rainbows. However, breeding rainbow trout are not common and are far less likely to be so as the state-of-the-art technology used in fish farms ensures that the majority of rainbows used for restocking are female – helpful because the male trout matures at a much earlier age and is therefore much more out of condition at spawning time.

Loch Fitty is a fly-only water for the majority of the angling season, which runs from the beginning of March until Christmas Eve. As the water warms up throughout the spring, a traditional Scottish cast of flies – including a Black Pennel, Kingfisher Butcher and a Kate McLaren – will take trout a foot or so below the surface. The fly-anglers of today have a wide selection of flies in their boxes to suit all the varying conditions that the Scottish climate can come up with. Cold, windy, blustery days when fly life is at a minimum are well provided for. This type of weather needs a lure or a reservoir pattern which is tied with a view to attracting feeding trout by its shape, colour and movement in the water, and not one imitating a fly or other particular form of underwater life. They are mostly – but not exclusively – flamboyant and garish in colour and are usually tied on a larger hook – a size 8 or 6 – and weighted on occasions so as to take the lure down to deeper water quickly. These weighted lures are difficult to cast and often upset the fly-anglers' casting technique. Most learn the hard way that this imbalance can make lures travel through the air at around 25 mph, and, if they get out of control, the unlucky angler may find the hook embedded in a hand, head or worst of all on the face. As a fishery manager, I see many brightly coloured hooks dangling from various parts of my customers' anatomy, and indeed, the local hospital out-patients department has become skilled in the extraction of these ornaments!

As autumn winds gather and the water temperature drops, the fly-angler finds his quarry more difficult to catch. At Loch Fitty, from about the third week in October until the Saturday before Christmas, the anglers are allowed to use any legal method to catch trout except live fish bait. This rule is to stop the introduction of any other species of fish into the loch other than by natural means. The baits and techniques used are many and varied and include maggot, worms, sweetcorn and spinning lures.

The work of a fishery manager is enjoyable and rewarding but it has its drawbacks. The normal day in the angling season begins early and as the summer days lengthen so the working day gets accordingly longer. An hour after dawn is the time to be out on the water, for that is when Loch Fitty is visited by that great, black feathered poacher, the cormorant. These seafaring birds come inland more and more these days as fishing in coastal waters becomes more difficult, and it is a sad fact that if left alone they could easily decimate a well-stocked trout fishery, whether the trout be brown or rainbow. And at the other end of the day I sometimes don't get finished until around midnight if the last angler stays late in the lodge, determined to go into every detail of catching his 3 lb trout. I always smile and listen attentively but sometimes I would rather lock up for the night and go to bed.

Today I am out slightly earlier than usual and the far end of the loch is not yet visible from the lodge. Through the orange glow, my eyes play tricks on me. Is that a man standing over by Cushet Wood – a poacher perhaps? I'd better get the fast boat ready for the morning patrol. Five minutes later I slowly pass the fish cages. A quick look confirms that everything is shipshape, so I head out past the breakwater. There they are in Mallard Bay! A flock of about 30 cormorants and more circling above, high in the sky. They have not seen me as the early sun is directly at my back and the westerly breeze does not allow them to hear the powerful throb of the 40 hp outboard engine.

All the birds settle on the water, so now is the time to move . . . and move quickly – range 1,000 metres; sun and wind good. I hit the throttle and the small rigid-hull inflatable jumps out of the water on to the plane – 0–30 knots in 15 seconds; 700 metres closing fast; 500 metres – they hear me and sit up in the water looking agitated; 250 metres – they start to panic trying to fly with feathers wet (it is a strain as the cormorant is a better swimmer and diver than flyer); 25 metres, accompanied by loud blasts on the horns – the frightened birds fly in all directions to escape. There are 43 this morning but they quickly disappear over the Blairadam Forest, heading for some other trout loch. At least their breakfast is not being served at Loch Fitty today.

I ease back the throttle and turn towards the rising sun. Cushet Wood is now on my left – oh yes, where was that poacher? Is he still there? Thankfully, he is on four legs and closely resembles a Hereford-Friesian bullock steadily eating the rushes. The thought goes through my head that the ideal way to poach would be to dress as a pantomime cow, but although poaching can be a problem, it is not as bad as that yet!

It is now 4.55 a.m. and back at the lodge the kettle is on for a quick brew up. One of the night watchers comes in for a cuppa; he too was fooled by the bullock, but otherwise, all was quiet throughout the small hours of the night. It is far too nice a morning to go back to bed for a little more shut-eye, so we chat as we get the boats ready for the anglers. All the outboard engines are refuelled and tested and all the boats bailed out. Charlie looks out a good early morning cast of flies as he has seen a good fish moving off the Bank o' Reeds and a Pheasant Tail Nymph might just do the trick. I am grateful to see him go out fishing because the cormorants will not return with a boat on the water . . . although Charlie is no ornithologist and once he chased a pair of grebes for half an hour or so, convinced they were the enemy.

It is now 9 a.m. and the car park is beginning to fill up. I open the gates. Mr Richardson telephoned to say that his fishing friend has called off and he wonders if Peter, our ghillie, is available for the day. On every stretch of water that is fished there are those who love to give advice on what to do and when to do it. Some eventually make it their occupation and it is a wise angler who takes five minutes to glean all the information from those in the know. Peter is a great character, full of wisdom and stories. One day in May he was out with a client when a brisk but warm wind was blowing across the loch. As he stood up to net a fish, his hat blew off into the loch – and the fish was netted – then the hat. Four times it happened in all until the client asked, 'Peter, why do you not tie down your hat with the flaps of your deerstalker? Is that not what they are intended for?'

'Yes, indeed, sir,' Peter replied, 'but I have never used them since 1983, the year of the great, great disaster.'

'What disaster?' the client thought, not wanting to show that he had no idea what Peter was talking about. Was it flood, storm or drought?

'It was the year on a cold March day that the laird offered me a dram and I never heard him!'

Ten o'clock is always a busy time, booking in the anglers for the day and discussing what the most productive tactics are likely to be. At Loch Fitty we have a 'Recommended Flies for the Day' blackboard which is written up each morning with advice on lines and hook sizes as well. One 1 April – a Sunday and, as usual at Loch Fitty, a late, sleepy morning – we advised a size 12 Kerr's Pink on the bob, teamed with an Orange Pippin, size 10 long shank, for the tail. It was amazing how many unsuspecting anglers were caught out and asked Argyll – who looks after the fly section of the tackle shop in the lodge – for these two flies which were new to them. Were they new patterns from the English reservoirs or had the local fly-tyers come up with some new ideas?

A tense moment at the weigh-in

It is now 11.00 a.m. and all the staff set out for the fish cages to grade trout for stocking the loch. At Fitty we stock twice a week in the summer months and this can mean around 1,500 trout a week at the peak of the season. The cage farm produces good quality trout and, because they are introduced to the loch at about six inches in length or 4 oz in weight, by the time they reach 1 lb 4 oz plus, they are well conditioned to their environment and require no settling-in period. In this way, we try to give the fish the best opportunity for acclimatisation and give the angler a good quality quarry.

Today it is hot, with the water temperature at 17°C, so speed is of the essence. It is a favourite job with all the staff as we are all anglers and pleased to see so many well-finned bars of silver going into the loch. If the anglers do not catch them, perhaps we will! As normal, the fish were spread over the water to give all areas an equal chance, although it is peculiar how certain parts of the loch always attract more. Something to do with the feeding, I suspect. We had one angler last week with a sonar device for fish detection which I would not permit him to take out on the water. As I see it, fishing is a day's relaxation in pursuit of the ever-elusive trout and, while we do our best to tell the angler where to fish, we are not in favour of these electronic gadgets.

We take the last tank of 250 trout up to Mallard Bay where the Meldrum Burn flows into the loch and as we approach the burn mouth I catch a glimpse of a bubble float hastily being retrieved into the willows we planted some five or six years ago. What a stupid colour to use for a float when poaching – hot orange! Ian takes the boat further up the burn and the chase begins. But it is only three young-sters of about 14 or 15 years of age who are very easily caught as they do not know the lie of the land and soon run into the marsh. We examine their bags and there are no trout, but in return for them we confirm their names and addresses. I think I know two of them and I am sure they will get their angling exploits curtailed when I visit their homes tonight.

Back to the lodge in good time for the day boats coming in. Mr Richardson has done well with his ghillie – has a nice basket of trout which turned the scales at 8 lb 14 oz, plus one small brown trout returned. Mr Maitland also has plump trout to weigh in but they are slightly heavier at 9 lb 3 oz. He is well pleased as he caught the majority on a self-tied green buzzer variant. It looks standard to me but he assures me that it was tied slightly differently from the normal buzzer and that this was the crucial factor in attracting the heavier trout.

The evening anglers are concerned about the wind but the Meteorological Office assures me that the wind will drop by 8 p.m. and now the club secretaries are happy to advise their members to go out. On days or evenings when the wind is strong and the anglers' flies are more often under the boat than out in front, it is advisable to use a drogue. A modern drogue is made from a very strong fabric – remarkably light and easily packed into the corner of a fishing-bag. When it is put into the water on the windward side of the boat it inflates into an underwater parachute, slowing down the drift of the boat and making it easier to fish. However, as one angler at Loch Fitty learned, they do have drawbacks. It was 5.30 p.m. and the evening fishers were leaving from the jetties. This particular angler was in the middle of the boat reaching for his drogue as the wind was freshening. The cord came out first and he wound it around his wrist when the drogue itself, which was neatly folded, suddenly inflated in the strongish wind. This, of course, pulled him downwind – unfortunately the boat was beginning to travel upwind – and as a result he shot straight out of the stern and into the water.

Luckily, at Loch Fitty the water 15 metres from jetty number one is about one metre deep and the only damage he did was to his pride. The rest of the angling club members appreciated this performance immensely, though. I always keep a dry change of clothing at the lodge so he was able to change quickly and return to his boat to the call of, 'Come on, Mary Poppins.'

Ian comes back on duty at 6.30 p.m. and he jokes about the drogue. I leave, saying that I will back about 10.00 p.m. to help with the boats coming in as there are 22 on the water tonight. My wife Lisa and I have supper together and then we do a little work in the garden. We live on the south east side of the loch. It is now a beautiful evening and the weatherman's prediction was most accurate as the wind has dropped away and I can see fish rising and nets dipping into the water. There will be some good returns tonight. Dave, a very regular angler at Loch Fitty, is out fishing this evening and looking for a lift home as his car is out of action. He is delighted with a 5 lb 12 oz rainbow he has tempted with a size 12 longshank Yellow Hopper. His wife recently met her friend at the supermarket.

'Ever since Dave took up fishing, he is hardly ever at home. He is out every other evening and away most weekends. When I do see him,' she said, 'he seems like a complete stranger.'

'How thrilling,' was the quick reply.

The chat in the lodge is full of stories of casting to rising fish and the gentle take of the larger fish feeding in the shallows. I tell the story of chasing the youngsters who were poaching the burn and the conversation soon turns to the law relating to angling for freshwater fish in Scotland. Many anglers are firmly of the opinion that, in Scotland, the right of trout fishing is public. In his helpful booklet, *Fishing in Scotland – Law for the Angler*, the Hon. Lord Jauncey, Senator of the College of Justice, states quite clearly that this is a misguided belief and is very far from being the case. The public at large have no right to fish for trout without permission. If a person fishes with rod and line for trout without permission of the proprietor, he may be turned off the water. He may also find himself liable civilly if he has caused damage and an interdict may be granted against him at his expense if there is reason to believe that he will continue to fish without permission. Furthermore, where a water has been artificially stocked with brown or rainbow trout it is probable that an angler who takes those fish without permission has committed theft.

It is a serious conversation, but the day ends as it began – with a welcome cup of tea. Those anglers with the bigger fish put them on the scales again – just to confirm how heavy they are, of course – and, as they leave, I hear the occasional impassioned prayer ascend into the night sky:

> God grant that I may catch a trout
> So big that even I
> When speaking of it afterwards
> May never need to lie.

CLYDE TIDE

Ricky Walker

Perhaps it's just kismet or fate, or maybe just sheer chance that of all the chapters in this book, the one which should fall to me is the one on inshore fishing. It was inshore fishing, or in my case, Firth of Clyde fishing, which first got me hooked on the sport, and ultimately *Hooked on Scotland*. It was inshore fishing which gave me my first tight line, and that real and enviable taste of success as far as catching anything worth keeping is concerned.

It all started in my schooldays. I would have been about nine or ten at the time, and, like many other Glasgow families, our annual holiday was two weeks doon the watter. Those were the days before package holidays, and Ibiza and Majorca still little more than fly-blown specks in an atlas. For us, as for almost everyone else, it was the Clyde Coast or nothing. Even so, the holiday island of Great Cumbrae and the colourful resort town of Millport were as exciting and magical to a small boy as anything the Balearics would offer later.

For me, Millport was as far off and distant as Treasure Island had been to young Jim Hawkins who would surely have recognised at least something familiar in our preparations. Everything you could possibly need for a fortnight, and a great many things that you wouldn't in a month of Sundays, were packed into a huge metal cabin-trunk which had to be manhandled the quarter of a mile to the local railway station. Once at Burnside station, the journey proper to this faraway resort would start, a journey which remarkably, even in 1958, could take the best part of a day. The steam train came peching and wheezing into Burnside before everyone piled in for the journey to Glasgow Central. Once in Glasgow, the cabin trunk was again pushed, pulled and cajoled the few hundred yards to St Enoch's station where we boarded another train bound for exotic points west; well, at least Fairlie's terminal, to catch the paddle steamer.

The PS *Talisman* was my first sight of an ocean-going vessel. To my young mind she was as handsome and elegant as any Cunarder, though she did little more than ply her trade from the mainland to Millport. That journey couldn't have taken more than fifteen minutes but to this latter-day Jim Hawkins, it seemed as if we might sail off the edge of the world. I was almost bursting with excitement and anticipation, fascinated by the vast expanse of what I took to be a mighty ocean but was only the Firth of Clyde, and entranced by the sight of the mighty paddles churning the waters and thrashing them into snow-white foam as the gulls wheeled overhead.

Getting off the boat and dragging the family and the trunk to the holiday home remains a blur to this day. What I can remember as though it were only yesterday, however, was the mad dash to Mapes, where I blew the bulk of my hard-saved and even harder-earned holiday money in as many minutes. Mapes is still there even now, and is still an Aladdin's Cave for fishermen young and old. It was there where I bought my first hand line complete with metal line spreader, hooks and weight.

With my new tackle, I would head for the pier or the rocks to spend many blissful but fruitless hours waiting for something other than crabs and coalfish to throw themselves on to my line. But, as I kept my solitary vigil, my attention was taken by the activities of the large wooden

Jim Brown with over 50 lb of tench

A cracker of a tope: 42 lb to Craig Wieland

A decent shore-caught codling

Fishing the South African surf

*On the pier at Loch Fitty with
Gerald MacKenzie*

*Iain Mackenzie and Ian Byrne of
Runrig ashore, with Bones
Gibson, David Burt and Ian
Galloway afloat*

Ferox bait!

Two ferox, 15 lb and 12½ lb, to the Ferox 85 group

Returning the 15-pounder to fight another day

Mike Maule with a fine Loch Awe pike of 33 lb

The 60-pounder about to be returned

Into that 140-pounder

Douglas 'Bugsy' Stewart – Tay

angling boat that was plying for trade trying to entice holiday-makers into an evening's line fishing out in the bay. It was six o'clock on a summer's evening, and the *Endeavour* – that was her name – was going out for a three-hour trip. I well remember looking on with boyish envy at the growing numbers of would-be fishermen as they carefully selected the hand lines which were kept in a box at the stern of the boat. Screwing my courage to the sticking point, I called down to the man in charge, a Captain Birds Eye lookalike I later came to know as Mr Hunter, and asked what the fare was and what time he came back.

'We're just out for the three hours tonight and the fare is three shillings with all your bait supplied,' came the enticing reply.

I thrust my hands deep into my pocket and rummaged around to pull out a handful of coins. Even after another search and countless recounts, I was devastated to learn that my worldly fortune amounted to the grand total of one and sixpence ha'penny. I was crushed. Mr Hunter was obviously able to read a good deal more than sea conditions, because taking one look at my crestfallen features, he told me it would be a good ten minutes before they set off so I would have time to go home and get some more money if I could.

I would have given Christopher Chataway a run for his money that night as I tore up the road from the pier to negotiate a short-term bridging loan from my family. As it happened, the fiscal negotiations hit a sticky patch fairly early on, since it transpired that my mum had had an evening meal on the table for a good half-hour and was not unnaturally a little peeved at my non-appearance. Even allowing for those unforeseen snags, I was still breaking records in spite of the pain in my side from bolting down a hurried dinner, as I ran down Richie Street back to the pier.

As I breathlessly rounded the corner, my heart sank. I had arrived just in time to see the *Endeavour* fully loaded with optimistic fishermen motoring round by the end of the pier on its way to the fishing. Fortunately, if nothing else, I was a resilient child and, not being one for dwelling on disappointments too long, I about-turned and strolled back up Richie Street for the ice-cream and fruit I had spurned but moments earlier on the grounds that I had gone off ice-cream for life.

Later that evening, back on the pier to continue my thankless thrash with the crabs and coalies, I watched as the *Endeavour* came into view in the distance. Trailing in the wake of the 40-footer, a mass of gulls like a cloud of giant midgies dived and twisted into her wash as she headed back to harbour. Their cries were indicator enough of a successful night's fishing, and so it proved.

I can remember vividly the sight of those nameless, faceless holidaymakers coming up the stone steps from the boat with strings of freshly caught sea fish; cod and haddock and pollack and beautiful big plaice with bright orange spots and creamy white underbellies. Everyone had taken a fish – even the young boy who, that very day, had told me he had never caught a fish in his life before, had a string of eight or nine plump haddock which he thrust triumphantly before me.

'Anything worthwhile from the pier?' he enquired snidely. I said nothing. I was simply mesmerised at the sight of this magnificent night's fishing.

It will come as no surprise to learn that the following evening saw me first in the queue for the *Endeavour*, fully funded for the three-hour excursion into what was, for me, the unknown. Even Mr Hunter could not help but be amused by my eagerness. For my part, I was convinced that, armed with that knowledge, he was making the journey out to fishing grounds agonisingly slow. All the more so since I had been baited up and ready to fish at least half an hour before we had even sailed. But at last the engine was cut and the anchor put over the side. My weight, line and cockle-baited hook dangled expectantly over the gunwales as we all waited for the skipper to give the signal.

Cool dude Ricky Walker with a Clyde catch

'Okay lads,' said the boatman, and a trembling hand let go the braided fishing twine, feeling its coarseness slip through my fingers. I watched as it disappeared into the depths. The water was shallower than I had expected, and the weight hit the bottom with a bump sooner than I would have thought. But now all was ready, and almost immediately cod and haddock came into the boat as they struck lines down below with lemming-like zeal. I became more anxious with each passing moment as I waited for a signal from the deep that something was interested in what I was offering. All of ten minutes passed, though it might have been hours, before I felt that wonderful pulling at the line. Gentle at first, almost tentative, then . . . I struck! I almost fell overboard as I hauled in the line, hand over hand, to retrieve my gleaming prize, a wonderful 3 lb cod. It was the first of many that night and, for me, the start of a love affair with inshore sea angling, which still takes me afloat whenever the chance presents itself. I have caught many fish since then, and a great many bigger than that first cod, but there has still as yet been nothing to match that first magical night aboard the *Endeavour*.

Like almost every other angler my attention was distracted in my teens by women and the need to find gainful employment, two aims which were not entirely unconnected.

So at the age of 21 I got the key of the door and with it, an invitation to become one of the men from the Pru – joining the Prudential Insurance Company as a very young agent. However, I did not know then that this was about to rekindle my passion for fishing thanks to a colleague called Donald Smart. I first noticed Don because of his attention to neatness and detail which was the exact opposite of my somewhat haphazard approach. Our regular Wednesday meetings at head office also yielded a mutual love for fishing and our love of the wide open spaces soon topped the agenda at almost every meeting.

Like myself, Don had a yen for sea angling and a few

weeks after we met he decided to buy a boat. True to form, he spent weeks getting quotes and examining all the ins and outs before he committed himself to a package deal comprising a 12-foot Skippy dinghy with road trailer, fenders and a two horsepower outboard. At last we could search for the big ones wherever we wanted, unfettered by the whims of the local charter boat owners; at last we could cast in any direction without the humiliation of having to untangle your lines from the 15 or 20 others on the boat. But our first liberating voyage of discovery was still a few weeks off as I was soon to discover.

It was another month in fact before Don pronounced himself ready to set sail. By that time the plain little dinghy had been transformed with the addition of navigation lights, cushions, a storage area for the anchor rope, brass fittings, carpets, and all manner of weird and wonderful compartments for stowing gear. It was everything you would have expected in a boat owned by Don.

That first morning we sped towards the coast at a steady 29 miles an hour but my mind was already racing with anticipation of what lay in store. Conditions were, to be truthful, a little less than perfect with a wind from the west at a steady 15 knots. As we arrived at Fairlie Beach I could see the odd white wave crest break as the wind gusted over it. Of course none of this was enough to diminish our enthusiasm as we unhitched the boat.

The first thing I noticed was how different a boat she had become with the extra weight from tackle, food and everything else. The second thing that struck me as we struggled and strained to get this lump of a boat over the soft sand was how far the tide goes out at Fairlie. I made a mental note to check that sort of thing next time. There was half an hour of pushing and shoving accompanied by the odd muttered oath before we finally reached the water's edge. As Don held Skippy to stop her being washed back ashore I struggled back up the beach making another mental note, this time about what little difference the absence of the boat made to the trailer when you are pulling it on your own.

Nevertheless we did finally make it into the water and the engine started first time – which I personally took to be an indicator of our good fortune. At full throttle we weren't exactly careering through the waves – it was more like a steady two or three knots, though the noise of the engine made it sound like we were auditioning for *Miami Vice*. Eventually Don's instinct told him we were at a likely spot and we dropped anchor.

Out of the rod bag came Don's gleaming rod and reel, and it was all I could do not to be overly impressed when he produced a cantilevered tackle box which was laid out like a supermarket. Everything was shiny and new and Don was obviously the sort who believed in a place for everything and everything in its place. Don was fishing and landing them before I had managed to find a service-able set of mackerel feathers from a small tackle bag full of odds and ends which hadn't been cleaned or even looked at since my last trip.

Probably more by luck than judgment we had anchored over a shoal of mackerel and we were pulling them in thick and fast. But after the initial euphoria had passed Don, to my surprise, started getting a little irate. The joy of fishing had now been surpassed by concern at the mess the fish were making as we brought them aboard.

We weighed anchor and went in search of less messy fish but every time we stopped we found ourselves catching these ill-mannered mackerel who, for some strange reason, thought nothing of messing up Don's boat in their death throes. Even with the aid of a bin bag the boat started to look less and less pristine with the arrival of every fish and Don was spending more time mopping and cleaning than fishing.

Worse was to come on the way back to shore. The wind had got up by now and the spray started to come into the boat, the neat little pieces of carpet began to float around, the comfy cushions quickly became sodden, and a silvery layer of fish scales covered the boat from one gunwale to the other.

Don was not a happy chappie when we finally put in at Fairlie. We had a good catch but for him eight weeks' work had been spoiled in large measure by the fish. From then on we only went out on really calm days, and only then when we had plenty of bin bags.

I fished with Don on and off whenever I could for about a year. Then due to promotion I moved down to Kilmarnock to take over a new agency, and it was there I met Bruce Robertson. Bruce was a very keen angler – any weather, any time, day or night, Bruce was your man – and we used to have some great forays on the Clyde. It was ideal. We both worked in insurance and because of the nature of our working week we always had Thursdays off. We would often leave before dawn and not return until the last bit of light had faded, in fact sometimes we used to fish long into the night depending on the weather. To be honest, though, the weather was hardly a factor: it could rain, it could snow, it could blow, as long as we were sheltered and as long as there were fish about to be caught, we'd be out there.

One of the most memorable times with Bruce was when we had been fishing for about two months and having various degrees of success and gaining more and more experience. With Don I had been fishing inshore for small fish like those messy mackerel. I knew, however, that there were some deeper marks and one particular winter Thursday I discovered them with a vengeance.

It was a very still quiet day, with little patches of sea fog in places. We arrived at the shore and as usual struggled across the sand with the boat; we didn't have trailers like today which can slip a boat; this was a home-made trailer which required a lot of muscle power. We launched successfully and after priming the engine we managed to get it running and headed off to some of the marks we usually fished over beside Kepple Pier. Kepple

That good Clyde cod – 20 lbs

was great because there is a nice rocky ledge and you could get red cod and wonderful pollack up to 5 or 6 lb on occasion.

We'd been drifting for about two or three hours catching these smaller fish when we decided to try out towards the main channel. We had fished this mark before and caught one or two nice cod up to about 4 or 5 lb. On the last occasion one cod, quite big, about 5 or 6 lb, had been caught on mackerel feathers just as the tide was on the turn. When the fish was boated it was found to have its mouth crammed full of lovely pink prawns. As we headed out from Kepple I noticed the sea fog getting thicker until eventually we lost sight of the shore. This wasn't a major problem because you can't go far in this area of the Clyde Estuary without hitting land of some description.

We dropped anchor where we thought we had been the last time. However, it was quite noticeable that we were paying out a lot more rope than usual. Eventually after drifting a little while the anchor took hold. The method we used for fishing at that time was what anglers call 'pirking'. A 'pirk' is a silver lure weighing about six or seven ounces, a shiny bar of metal with a treble hook attached to the bottom. Above the pirk we fished two or three mackerel feathers so that any small fish that didn't want to take the bait on the pirk could be caught on the feathers. Our method, such as it was, was to drop anchor and let the boat settle on the tide which ran there like a slow moving river. The idea being to cast up against the tide and as the lure was sinking perhaps 70 or 80 feet, it would come down with the tide and by the time it hit the bottom you'd be fishing almost vertically with the lure. You could then jog the lure up and down pirking, and as you moved it the lure would drift slowly backwards with the tide until it got so far away from the boat you had to retrieve it then cast back up again.

The water was flat calm, with only the sound of the odd seagull wheeling above, and the splash into the calm water

Evening settles across the Clyde Estuary

as I cast my lure up tide into the mist. I couldn't actually see the lure hitting the water, but I could just hear it plop and then watch the line feed out from my reel. We had settled in this mark, casting up-tide, and feeling the lure hit the bottom as the line went slack and then you'd start pirking, just lifting and dropping until the lure would be fishing right under your feet but this day as the line passed the back end of the boat the rod just went solid. Now the biggest fish I had caught up till this time was a 6 or 7 lb cod and when it went solid I thought we'd obviously hit some snag because we were aware there was some rough ground about. But then the snag started to move and the line started pulling off the reel!

The rod bent and I leaned into it, and when I felt the pounding I knew this was something substantial. I'd never felt anything as heavy as this on my line. Suddenly the line went slack and the fish was off. Quickly I reeled in the pirk to cast again when Bruce, who was fishing on the opposite side of the boat, let out a scream and his rod buckled over: he was hard into a big fish as well. I watched him trying to strain at his rod and eventually the fish started to come up and within a couple of minutes he had boated a beautiful cod. It was a magnificent fish, green back, superbly conditioned, and weighing 20 lb. For us landing a fish such as this was like running a four-minute mile.

By this time I was just letting my lure come down the tide again and was so stunned with Bruce's success I didn't even bother pirking. I then realised that my rod was down too, and as I lifted it I felt my rod bending over and a few minutes later I brought in a fish which was 25 lb. As the 25-pounder came over the side it coughed up bright orange prawns. Obviously the fish down there were just gorging themselves on the prawn beds which we were fortunately sitting on top of. Within an hour we had caught another three or four decent sized fish – nothing quite as big as the first two but all of them came out with prawns. As the tide slackened, the fish started to disappear, or we stopped getting bites, but we kept trying.

The mist cleared and to our great surprise, we found ourselves at least a mile away from the mark we had originally aimed for. We must have actually been drifting slightly and had taken anchor on this haven for big fish.

It was about ten days before we actually managed to get back out to fish. By this time we'd told a couple of friends and they were all keen to come with us. We took another trip and a third trip after that. I remember as soon as we got there, dropping the anchor to start fishing but we never caught a thing, moving again, trying to line up what we thought were these marks. It's funny really with inshore fishing you've got to be right on the nose. That day we moved about three or four times, before we made contact with those big heavyweight cod, and again that day we had half a dozen. I think the biggest one was well over 25-30 lb, really wonderful, wonderful inshore Clyde fishing.

After about 12 months of regular success Bruce and I decided to combine our day jobs with weekend charter work so we could share this wonderful fishing with more enthusiasts. So we started looking for a boat big enough to do charter work thus combining fun with a bit of income, and possibly extend our fishing time as well. Or at least that was the theory.

We travelled the length and breadth of Scotland until we discovered a boat for sale that was within our price range and was the size we needed. Aptly named the *Cumbrian*, she was a wooden boat, 32 ft long, and had formerly been a pinnace. A pinnace is the boat the seniors used to go to and from land to the main ship. She had nice lines and although she'd seen her best she was certainly serviceable. The only major problem we could see about was that the boat had a hand crank engine – an old Kelvin diesel/diesel paraffin engine with four cylinders. What a performance to try and start it! You had to fill four cups located on the top of the engine next to the intake manifold with paraffin, then you had to throw a de-compression lever. Then as you swung the cranking handle you had to keep your thumbs well clear because if it kicked back it could take your arm off. Once you got the momentum going on this huge fly wheel, you then flicked over the compression lever and eventually it would splutter and cough into life running first on paraffin then, when it warmed up, you could switch over to diesel.

It was a superb old engine and, looking back, probably the easiest thing we could have done was to have it serviced and put an electric starter on it. But the engine was our only problem and the asking price for the *Cumbrian* was £1,200, which I thought was quite reasonable. But because the engine was a hand start we got her for £1,000!

I still remember the sense of pride and the glowing satisfaction when the transaction was complete and we headed out through the harbour mouth at Ardrossan and set course for Irvine which was to be our base to refurbish the *Cumbrian*. Our estimated time for repairs was around two and a half months; we had already earmarked a modern diesel engine and apart from replacing the radiator with a heat exchanger and additional piping little more than cosmetic changes remained to be made to smarten her up for the coming season.

Five months later and with the highlight of the season – the Arran Sea Angling festival – looming ever closer we were still having what we euphemistically referred to as teething problems. The Arran festival is the oldest in Scotland and attracts to the island a Dunkirk-like armada of small boats to augment the local fleet and take the anglers out for the weekend's fishing. It may have been Arran's version of Dunkirk but for us it was D Day.

By working every hour God sent us, (apart from the minimum time we could decently give to the Prudential), though, we were all ready – with the exception of a minor niggle concerning the fan belt when the morning of the festival finally dawned. Put simply, the minor niggle meant that, despite our best efforts the fan belt resolutely refused to stay on. The belt was vital since it not only turned the actual generator but it also fed the engine with sea water for the cooling system. Without it the engine would overheat and cut out, leaving us with no means of propulsion.

We searched frantically, scouring every garage, scrap-yard and chandlers we could find to get a belt that would fit, all the while watching with anguish as the other Irvine boats sailed for Arran. Although we were frustrated we were not too distressed because Arran was after all only 18 miles due west and once we set off it would be plain sailing. Or so we thought.

Eventually we found an adjustable fan belt which appeared to do the job, allowing us to finally set off around tea time. We cast off our land lines and headed into a nice friendly night with me at the helm and Bruce keeping an anxious eye on the fan belt, pausing only to give me an optimistic thumbs up from time to time. The third member of our happy band, George Armstrong, lounged luxuriously in the back of the boat taking the early evening air. God was in his heaven and all seemed well with the world until we got about ten miles out, just past the point of no return.

Bruce by this time had relaxed his vigilance on the troublesome fan belt as had we all; however, it recaptured our attention when we heard a dull thud. It was a sound we had heard many times before; the sickening announcement that yet another fan belt had departed. By this stage we were well versed in the ways of repairing fan belts and it seemed only the work of a moment to cut the engine and make yet another running repair. In fact, the running repairs turned into a gallop as we put the belt together three more times before it finally gave up the ghost altogether and fell into several pieces which could never be put together again. At this stage Arran was only some eight miles away but as the dusk gathered the beam from the lighthouse at Holy Isle became a beckoning beacon. We knew that once we had rounded it we would be relatively safe in sheltered waters, but without the cooling system the engine could only run for about ten minutes at a time before it had to be switched off to cool down. During its cooling off period we would then be at the mercy of the current and the deteriorating weather conditions which combined to eat up whatever progress we made. To add to our problems this system took its toll on the battery since without the fan belt it could not be recharged from the engine.

Drifting in the formerly friendly Clyde Estuary in pitch darkness with only one light tantalisingly close but no way of getting to it certainly provides a very real sense of your own mortality and an almost religious understanding of your insignificance in the great scheme of things. It wasn't

The Cumbrian – *before her refit!*

life-threatening yet, but who knew what the night would bring.

But moments of blind panic frequently provide insights of equally blinding clarity. We knew as we heard the sickeningly slow sound of the engine turning over that this would be our last chance. If we had been driving a car along a dark road it would have been a simple case of fetching jump leads and a willing neighbour – but this was an entirely different situation. Almost miraculously the engine did kick into life one last time but looking at the remaining flicker of the navigation lights which had once burned bright we knew this would be its last gasp.

Then inspiration struck and Bruce came up with what he admitted was a daft suggestion. 'Why don't we just chuck buckets of water over the damn thing,' he said with a note of hopeless desperation. I instantly dismissed this forgetting that, unlike a petrol engine, a diesel had no electrical spark which could be doused by water. In fact, apart from issuing great clouds of angry steam, the engine would be unharmed by the process although it could only be kept going fairly slowly.

We stripped off the engine casing and tentatively tried a few experimental buckets and were delighted to see the temperature guage move slowly out of the red. A human chain was set up with buckets of water broken only by my frequent forays to the hand bilge pump to keep us afloat. Although I wouldn't recommend it to anyone else for fear of cracking the cylinder block, we were lucky and this Heath Robinson arrangement saw us around the Holy Isle lighthouse and safely into Lamlash at three in the morning. We knew we were in sheltered waters even if we didn't know where and were happy to drop anchor and collapse in an exhausted sleep.

When dawn broke we found ourselves about a mile away from the other boats which wasn't bad navigation under the circumstances. Although we couldn't fix the engine ourselves we found a man who could, and instead of spending the weekend fishing we spent it on repairs.

The trip back was happily uneventful but the baptism by fire taught me a lot of lessons. Since then I have never ventured out without first checking that mechanically everything is as it should be. On that initial (near disastrous) trip to Arran in the *Cumbrian* I learned a valuable lesson about boat safety that has stayed with me to this day. And that is, safety at sea is not a luxury: it's vital and the inshore boat angler must always be aware that little problems which would be simple to remedy on land can, at sea, develop into potential life-threateners.

Competent inshore anglers have a great respect for the sea. They know the capability of their craft, they're able to recognise and anticipate deteriorating weather conditions and know when to stay and when to run for home. Of course, before setting out all mariners or boat anglers should furnish themselves with an up-to-date weather forecast for their area and should have a check-list covering the following: sufficient fuel for the trip; charts for the waters they intend to fish; a secondary means of pro-pulsion like oars or a small outboard motor; a bailer or bucket; proper warm, water-proof clothing; a means of attracting attention like flares etc. in case they do run into real problems.

And always remember Murphy's first law of seafaring – *whatever can go wrong will go wrong and at the worst possible time!*

Safety is important but don't let this put you off going fishing. I can think of nothing better on a mild summer's evening than heading out for some serious inshore boat angling and, although nowadays the fish are scarcer than in days gone by, there is a lot more to fishing than just fish. There is the thrill of anticipation, watching your line and trace disappearing down into the depths, followed moments later by the contact with the sea-bed as your baited hook and line explores an unseen world below.

Above, in the boat, you relax – gently bobbing and rolling, the panoramic view of the evening sky with its graduation colours, mirrored a shade darker in the moving sea. As you drift, the problems of life dissolve into obscurity and time almost stands still as you bask in the gentle atmosphere of calm. Then, like an alarm clock you feel that gentle tug-tug on the rod, your senses become sharp, you wait for the bite to develop, not knowing if that signal from below is from a six-ounce Dab or just maybe, the fish of a lifetime!

SWIMMING PAST THE SCOTCH MYTHS

Ron Greer

'An ugly-looking, toothy "tadpole" of a fish. Dark, fierce, cannibalistic and no sport in catching one. Maybe worth a bash for if it's flat calm and nothing else is on. A Victorian myth that isn't worth considering today.'

These are the words or sentiments that seem to sum up the attitude of many ordinary anglers to ferox brown trout. Even their very name conjures up tribal demons from our stone-age past. Only that other fish predator, the pike, engenders the same emotive response at the mention of its name. Say the word 'ferox' even slightly louder than normal in an angler-frequented pub and more often than not you will be the subject of quizzical glances. Perhaps the response to the word belongs to the same part of the human psyche as wolf, shark, and bear. Just like these animals, ferox are misunderstood and undervalued both in their own right and in what they have to offer human beings. Often myth and prejudice take the place of informed knowledge and reason when those people who have little direct contact with the animal air their views. Those who know more, seldom speak so negatively.

There is of course, a flip-side to this negative 'predator response' in human beings. Strangely enough, the more positive approach tends to come not just from the 'save

Ron Greer keeps an eye on that rod top

the cuddly teddy bear' subculture but from the very fortunate people engaged in pursuit of the predator. Far from
having an atavistic attitude to their quarry, true hunters –
especially sporting ones – tend to develop deep reverence
and respect for it: in fact, almost a love of the animal they
pursue.

After all, tiger conservation owes much to that famous
killer of man-eaters, Jim Corbett, who, although spending
a lifetime despatching tigers that had become a threat to
people, understood that these cats and the environment
that supports them are of value, not only in their own
right, but to the world as a whole.

It is a similar story in the angling world. We are all well
aware of carp- and pike-specimen hunters who have spent
much of their lives studying the one fish that really makes
them tick, as angler and human being. They defend most
rigorously not only the privilege to fish for them, but also
the right of the fish to continued existence in an environment suitable for it. There is an undoubted fascination with
ferox which has some of its roots in the comity of angling's
psychological scenario.

Nevertheless, ferox fascination also derives much of its
holding power from the very environment and its special
place in Scottish history and culture. I am, of course,
talking about the Highlands, for it is here that the vast
majority of ferox populations in the British Isles exist and
naturally enough, most of the British populations of arctic
charr as well. All predators need a prey and in the case of
ferox, this is mainly its smaller Ice-Age cousin.

Charr probably have as many myths associated with
them as ferox, the main one being that they are rare. This is
simply not the case at all. There are quite literally hundreds
of populations of arctic charr in the Highlands. Indeed,
some lochs even contain two strains of charr – a case of
ferox being spoiled for choice! On top of that, the physical
appearance of charr can vary considerably from loch to loch
even within the same drainage system and this has led to

a great deal of intense scientific debate over its genetic significance and how it arose. Relative positions in the debate are held with all the tenacity of rival supporters at an 'Old Firm' match. If it wasn't enough to argue over how many spots on a charr's flank constitute the next scientific treatise, there is even controversy over the spelling of its very name. Apparently, the whole thing started through a tiff between two famous fish classificationists in the late 19th century, who spelled the name differently from each other in an academic wind up that went over the top and has bored their successors for more than a century. Now the human race is only really divided into two groupings: those who spell the name 'charr' and those who spell it 'char' (although there are rumours of long-lost tribes in Buchan who use a third 'r'!). However, the general consensus is tending towards accepting 'charr' as the correct form, just as 'parr' is accepted for young salmon. As far as is known though, ferox do not ask the charr their spelling before devouring them, and are completely unconcerned about numbers of spots and gillraker counts. Amen.

Mentioning the Ice Age and including the word 'arctic' in the name of a fish explains the Highland connection neatly. No description of the natural history of the Scottish Highlands can avoid using the terms 'arctic' or 'sub-arctic' in summarising some aspect of the biology of wildlife. Much of the land lying above 1,000 feet has a climate broadly similar to Reykjavik in Iceland, and the Cairngorm car park offers weather that would make a citizen of Tromso, North Norway, feel quite at home.

The ferox connection is, in fact, an Ice-Age connection. We are dealing with something ancient here, a part of our collective glacial past that is still alive, yet capable of being accessed directly. At the close of the last Ice Age many large forms of animals existed, particularly large mammals. Collectively, these are known as the ice-age megafauna.

While huge bull reindeer battled for herd supremacy on the shores of what is now Loch Shin, and the 'great

Caledonian bear' was devouring an unlucky moose on what later became Flanders Moss, ferox and charr were enacting their own part of the drama – one that is fortunately still on stage. In a sense ferox are the last of that ice-age megafauna. It is indeed a privilege to be able to fish for them and to do so in an environment like the Highlands. If we were to lose them then we would lose a part of the very soul of angling in Scotland. Ferox are worth the bother even if you don't fish for them or have never even seen one. They are very large, long-lived brown trout which feed mainly on other fish, a description that belies the complexity of the argument which surrounds the questions of their ecology and genetics. Essentially this boils down to the hoary old problem of whether it is nature or nurture that produces the outcome, or, in this instance, both – a justifiable position to adopt until the scientific answers are more definitive. Dr Niall Campbell in both his scientific publications on ferox and in popular articles over the years has indicated that these predators are normally associated with a special set of environmental conditions. Normally they occur in relatively large lochs (over 100 hectares) which are biologically rather unproductive but do contain arctic charr. In these conditions they exhibit the archetypal ferox growth pattern of a slow period, perhaps for one-third of their lifetime, followed thereafter by very rapid growth leading to a size much above the general run of ordinary trout. In more productive lochs, trout generally tend not to have this type of growth pattern. The critical length for the change-over in growth is around 35 cm (14 inches) because in an unproductive loch, with rather low quantities of insect larvae and snails and so on, it probably becomes biologically uneconomical for a fish of this size to meet its food requirements. It is then left with the option of starving or switching to an alternative food source. And this is where the arctic charr come into the picture.

Charr are efficient harvesters of water fleas, pea mussels and midge larvae – items of food which cannot support the growth of ferox (directly) but which can support abundant small charr, the link in the food chain eventually leading to large trout. Unlike mammals, fish can continue to grow throughout their entire lives provided a convenient food supply exists and disease or parasites don't intervene. Thus, potential ferox can almost afford to wait several years in an insect-eating 'apprenticeship' before reaching a size which forces – or indeed, facilitates – the switch to a charr-eating diet. Ferox also supplement their food with frogs, seasonal newts and salmon smolts and, of course, they are not averse to devouring their smaller kin. Fish-farm escapee smolts and rainbow trout must be welcome 'suckers' to more wily wild prey and it's not unusual to find small mammals in the stomach of a ferox. I once found a six-inch charr and two voles while examining the stomach contents of one 3 lb ferox. And whilst working with some Norwegian colleagues at Lake Tunhovd in southern Norway I had the lunchtime pleasure of watching huge trout rising to lemmings swimming on their suicidal journey to oblivion. Examination of their stomachs indeed revealed a testimony to greed and opportunism. They seem to prefer prey of about a third of their own body length and are capable of devouring several fish of this size in a single feeding session. In fact, fish of half their own size can be consumed without too much concern it seems. On that same visit to Norway we looked at the stomach contents of a 19 lb ferox which contained nine charr of 8–10 inches in length. Faced with facts like this, one wonders if a Blair Spoon or a 28 g Toby is actually enticing enough!

There is also evidence to suggest that the fish-eating propensity of ferox is an inherent factor rather than one merely caused by random chance. Not apparent in all, or even the majority of the rest of the trout population, most brown trout will occasionally eat other fish to some extent. My colleagues, Jon Kristjansson in Iceland and Per Aass in Norway, have carried out a wide range of field-stocking trials assessing the performance of trout of different parental origins. Trout of ferox origin maintained their fish-eating habits when transferred to other mountain lakes containing charr, and sometimes 'out performed' the local inhabitants. On the other hand, Tunhovd-origin ferox, much in demand in Norway for stocking in lakes with large populations of stunted charr, did not do well in waters containing powan or vendace as fodder, while ferox actually derived from waters rich with these fish thrived although they did not compare favourably in charr waters. Similar trials in Scotland await implementation, though they have been under consideration for quite some time, funding being the usual problem.

Closer to home Dr Andrew Ferguson of Queens University Belfast has indicated clear genetic differences between ferox and other types of trout in Lough Melvin in Ireland. Whether the results of Scandinavian and Irish research can be extrapolated to Scotland remains to be seen. Past and on-going genetic research by my colleagues Dr Alistair Stephens, West Galloway Fisheries Trust, and Andrew Walker of the Freshwater Fisheries Laboratory, Pitlochry, may offer some guidance. I for one would place my bet on a strong genetic distinction being clarified in Scottish ferox too.

Perhaps by now you are convinced that in ferox we have a very special animal indeed. No doubt the more open-minded anglers among you are chomping at the bit to get started. Others of the 'grab a quick whopper brigade' will be nursing their short-sighted greed till their first day off. Dedicated fly fishermen have likely enough turned to the next chapter already. I hope any piscatorial poseurs among you who boast about catching tame rainbow trout on a 'dead budgie' pretending to be a pantomime fly have been embarrassed enough not to entertain comparing what you do with angling for a real big fish!

Ferox angling is about catching a wild fish in its natural wild habitat, not about catching some artificially reared dumbo that's never had to hunt for its dinner in its life.

Trolling for ferox

You never know in a wild loch what size of trout you might catch, let alone be aware that a record-breaker was put in five minutes ago. This is what real fishing is about, the promise, the uncertainty and the chance of a lifetime. It's the fond memories of occasional victories – or even more often bittersweet reflections on what might have been – that really make it all worth while. And in the end the integrity of the struggle becomes a victory in itself.

Catching ferox is certainly not easy – thank goodness. And no, you're not going to get a dot-to-dot guide within these pages. All the basic knowledge you require is readily available in angling books, periodicals and articles. Like the fish, these take a bit of seeking out, but in the end are well worth the effort, while any pike, salmon or carp angler worth his salt will probably already possess the basic equipment and the beginnings of the correct mental attitude. Some general advice, however, will be forthcoming, the real value of which will be vindicated if you ignore it!

First of all, concentrate on quality. You are never going to get very many in a season, no matter how good you become, so if your pleasure comes from catching dozens of escapee rainbows or bags of mackerel don't even start. Quality tackle is a must, expecially hooks and line, and while there is no need to use stiff rods, you should remember that you are after a very powerful fish that will test any weak links. A carp rod, light pike or salmon-spinning rod will do nicely, and longer, 10–12 foot rods are an advantage over shorter ones both for handling the fish and keeping the lines apart whilst trolling. You can catch ferox from the bank very successfully, but by and large pursuit is by boat. Again a good boat is essential, and unfortunately many of the boats available for hire on Highland lochs are not up to the rigours of trolling in a gale. If you do have any doubts about the safety of the boat, don't venture out and certainly not without a life-jacket. Determination is one thing, a death wish is something else. And once you have assured yourself that you have the best quality rod, line and reel that you can afford, not to mention protective clothing adequate for a sub-arctic session, you then have to ask yourself about the personal qualities required. For ferox, you will need mettle of a steely determination superior even to the metal of the best Partridge outpoint treble. You will have to be relentless, for you will be faced with more than a few days which seem like a bum-numbing, brain-numbing fishless eternity. And always choose your angling compadres with care, if possible making sure that it's not your turn to drive, for by this time you should have acquired a supply of top-quality malt whisky – cask strength is best, and an essential component of the après-ferox cultural exchange and post-blank-day recovery. Indeed in our Ferox 85 Group we have gone to the length of procuring our own special blend because, despite years of harsh experience, we still get many blank days.

Forget the rumours about size not being important. It is almost everything in ferox fishing, if not in romance – and so, of course, is quality. In angling for ferox, you will certainly find both. Far from ferox being the awful monstrosities of misguided popular myth, if you are fortunate enough to catch a late-summer fish which has not spawned in the previous season, you will have the pleasure of seeing a wild trout of the highest calibre. A huge American football with fins was the description I coined on seeing my first Norwegian ferox. A gob-smacking 24 lb of firm fighting-fit hen fish which was a far cry indeed from the flabby rotund floppiness of a recently released, finless-wonder stockie. And the quality of the Scottish ferox is no less than their Norwegian counterparts, although the official rod-caught record is still begging for a Scottish fish in excess of 20 lb. No doubt it will come. We know of four fish in the last ten years, regrettably not taken on rod and line, that were all well over 20 lb and there is also a very reliable report of a ferox considerably over 25 lb. We know the locale too – but needless to say, I'm not going to tell you. However, the quality of the ferox experience is not limited to the fish itself. Pursuit can take you to some of the most impressive scenic areas of the country and enable you to enjoy and absorb other aspects of Scotland's wildlife. As a tree lover, I find it enthralling slowly passing loch shores whose hillside above or, islands within, are bedecked in the last remnants of The Great Wood of Caledon. It is a sobering thought indeed to consider that both ferox and charr were present in the lochs concerned many centuries before the first woody plants could have grown large enough to provide our hunter-gatherer ancestors with tent poles. I wonder if ferox were ever on the menu of our paleolithic predecessors? If not, then they certainly missed out on an excellent culinary experience for ferox, at their best, rival – indeed exceed – most salmon and sea trout in providing a quality meal. We encourage, but do not insist on a catch-and-release policy on our outings, leaving the final choice to the individual. As native Caledonians, we consider ourselves as entitled as an Inuit or a Sami to dine on the anatomy of our native faunal resources, occasionally. This, of course, does not mean abusing the privilege, nor surrendering to an urban coffee-table, green morality. To baulk at killing such a magnificent animal is, of course, readily understandable and, as the capture of large trout becomes fairly frequent in a good season, it is amazing how much easier it becomes to return them. A case of familiarity breeding compassion, perhaps?

By 'we', I mean the Ferox 85 Group, set up in 1985 by the rare mixture of professional biologists and experienced loch anglers to continue the pursuit of what surely must be the mightiest of our permanently resident freshwater game fish. Ferox fishing will hopefully not become a mass participant sport. It takes a resolve and relentlessness not many people have and those that do thoroughly deserve their fish. On several occasions I've seen experienced trollers reduced to fly-fishing after several 12-hour days of nothingness only to see those who stuck it out with the correct set-up have a flurry of activity that not only changes their weekend but their angling lives. We don't despise fly fishermen, for they are a useful source of bait and any-one hooked on Scotland's angling scene deserves some brotherly respect. But so does our quarry. It is the top native fish predator in many Highland lochs and will only be available if the whole ecosystem which supports it is allowed to maintain its integrity. We borrow our ferox fishing from the next generation and in turn we have received an inheritance directly from the Ice Age. We might not find the Holy Grail whilst pursuing ferox but if we did, we would be guilty of not taking ferox angling seriously enough.

Treat any success you have as reward in itself, for the very people who initially doubted that your approach would be correct, will be among the first to exhibit the jealous bigotry of angling that only religion or politics can exceed. Catch one double-figure ferox and you might at best be considered an eccentric. Catch several, and you will be considered a dangerous eccentric – that is, unless you offer to take those who condemn you on a ferox hunt! Don't even think about entering your catch in any of the weekly or monthly award schemes run by the angling or daily press. In any case, the record you might catch isn't produced daily. It's something that might be 20 years in natural production.

We in Ferox 85 console ourselves on blank days with the thought that in the time taken to read this section, somewhere in Scotland a 30 lb ferox has just eaten the umpteen millionth ¾ lb charr since the glaciers departed.

Perhaps the umpteen millionth-and-one, will be the one with our hooks in it!

ESOX LUCIUS SCOTICUS MAXIMUS

Mike Maule

The float bobbed, almost imperceptibly, on the glossy surface of the lake. The young angler tensed as again the float moved, this time more positively. Then, with a distinct sense of purpose, the float slid beneath the surface.

The little boy struck the fish and battle was enjoined. A few moments later a 6 oz perch lay at his feet. With its spines defiantly erect and flanks shimmering, reflecting reds, olive green, brown, it was a miniature picture of perfection.

I suspect that this first encounter with the 'art of the angle' will have been repeated many times across the country and confirmed yet another angler to his sport. I also suspect that for many of us the bold, piratical perch will have obliged as that first fish.

For me, roach became my next quarry. Requiring much more finesse and delicate presentation, the roach is the 'sheep' of the fish world. Shy, retiring and delicate, it is the principal prey fish for many a predator.

Then one day, whilst reeling in yet another small roach, everything became solid. The line suddenly went slack and a big boil of water appeared on the surface. With a quick flick of its tail the 'submarine' contemptuously took my roach, my terminal tackle, the lot, to the bottom of the lake.

This fired my imagination. In my dreams the fish took on enormous proportions and I determined to catch the monster. The next day saw me back at the lake armed with an array of spinners, true to Mr Crabtree tradition, and I began my quest for the fearsome *Esox lucius* – the devil fish – or pike.

Success was some time coming, though, but eventually I was rewarded for my efforts with 5 lb of green 'muscle and teeth'. So began my fascination – my wife calls it obsession – with the pike, which some 30 or so years later continues with undimmed enthusiasm.

Few fish have attracted so much attention in folklore as the pike. Its reputation extends to 'dog eating', 'swan swallowing', a fish the size of crocodiles attacking small children who are silly enough to go swimming. None of this, of course, has a factual base. After all, the pike is only a fish.

Nevertheless, what is certain is that its reputation for *denuding* waters of other fish has caused it to be despised by both match and game anglers alike. Great efforts, and money, are expended by owners to rid their water of them which in most cases is wasted. Pike are part of the natural food chain and will find their own balance in the eco-system without man's interference. For this reason, I, and the vast majority of dedicated pike anglers, will return fish alive and unharmed to the water. What follows in this chapter will hopefully encourage the reader to do the same and keep the dream of that huge predator alive.

THE SCOTTISH PIKE
Pike are well distributed throughout Scotland from the Highlands to the Borders. Even the most barren-looking of lochs in areas like Wester Ross can turn up the odd surprise. However, as a general rule, the less acidic and richer the lochs, the more abundant and bigger the fish – making Loch Lomond, Loch Ken and Castle Loch (Lochmaben) much better bets for the serious pike angler. Loch Awe has also rightly gained a reputation as a big pike loch, but this

is in no small part due to the high number of escaped rainbow trout there – easy pickings for a hungry fish.

Having fished extensively in England, the general quality of Scottish pike seems to be superior. They fight like tigers and appear to be leaner and fitter than their English counterparts. This is probably due to the fact that Scottish pike have to hunt their prey rather than wait for a passing bream shoal as in the south. Whatever the reason, though, most visiting English anglers will agree that the fighting quality of a Scottish pike far exceeds what they experience in England, which, when taken with the wonderful scenery, makes Scottish piking a much more enjoyable experience.

PIKE LOCATION

When faced with a vast expanse of water it is quite a daunting prospect. Where are you likely to find pike? Without prior knowledge of the water, I would always start with a river inflow or outflow. These areas often have shallows around them and I look for areas with depths of around 2–12 feet. If there are weed-fringed areas, all the better.

Mike Maule's well-organised boat

Other likely areas include islands, shallow bays, areas showing fallen trees and weed- or lily-beds. If a boat is available, then it is worth the time and effort plumbing the areas for drop-offs (where the bottom falls away) – the favourite haunt of pike. Nevertheless, if local knowledge is available then it is often well worth a chat to game anglers to see if any have been caught. Most will readily give information if asked the right way.

I'm afraid I cheat! My boat is equipped with a fish-finder type echo sounder which gives a visual display of the bottom of the loch, pinpointing shoals of food-fish. The pike will not be far away. This particular piece of equipment has proved invaluable in sorting out likely fish-holding areas in lochs like Lomond. Boat fishing is a specialised art, though, and warrants a book in its own right.

LOCH AWE

We featured Loch Awe when filming *Hooked on Scotland*. Murphy's law intervened and fish were hard to come by. Over the years the loch has proved consistent for producing fish, although not many of any size until recently when rainbow trout escaped in vast numbers following winter storms. Indeed, it also contains good sized shoals of perch, charr and native brown trout, while salmon, sea trout and eels also run in the water. There are also extensive shallows and pike holding features – all the ingredients for quality pike water.

At the risk of self-indulgence, in fact, I will relate to you the story of my biggest pike to date. My friend Graham Burr and myself set off from Edinburgh on a wet and windy August morning to arrive at Loch Awe only to find the weather had worsened. No matter. Having made the effort, the determined angler is not put off by small things like that!

Stumbling through the peat bogs to reach the bank, I chose a swim adjacent to islands whilst Graham elected for a deeper swim close to an extensive reed-bed. The loch was high and rising. As light gathered, we saw the extent of the flooding and also the effect of the wind as it whipped the water into a white capped frenzy. First things first – I pitched my umbrella in a vain effort to get some shelter. I then cast out three rods secured to my rod-rests with bands to keep them in place.

For once everything went nicely to order. I made breakfast and was quite comfortable when I got my first run. A mid-double, which fought deep and hard. The action was consistent and by mid-afternoon I had had four double-figure pike to 18 lb. The wind had not abated but the rain was now patchy although, when accompanied with the strong wind, was still very unpleasant.

It was in the middle of one of these squalls when my middle rod developed a scorching run. An immediate strike and the fish was on. This time the pike decided to head straight out into the main loch. For a while I was forced to give line, despite all my efforts to stop the fish without risking a break – 15 lb line can take some punishment before it will actually snap. Then the fish decided to come towards me. I reeled in quickly to keep in contact with it, and for some 15 minutes it ploughed back and forth in front of me before finally tiring. Eventually we saw it. I realised that it was huge and I was very wary about applying too much pressure. To lose a pike like this so close to netting would have been heart-breaking.

Graham netted the fish with aplomb (thank goodness) and we both gasped in awe at the sheer size of it. At 33 lb it was perfect in every way. As with so many Scottish pike, the most impressive feature was the breadth of its back. (The crocodile myth sometimes looks real after all.)

Summer morning: Kilchurn Castle, Loch Awe

What was interesting about that day, though, was that I landed five other doubles and lost one other good fish. All had come to one rod, with no runs at all to the others. Graham, no more than 30 yards away, had blanked. This happens too often to be a coincidence. The pike sometimes seem to be tightly packed and baits must be presented in exactly the right place to get runs. Quite why this should happen I don't know. If you are in the right place at the right time you will get fish. The more you fish the more likely you are to be in the right place. But you will inevitably get your share of blank days.

LOCH LOMOND

This loch has to be the mecca of pike anglers – the home of the British record pike – 47½ lb caught by Tommy Morgan. If Loch Awe has the essential ingredients to be a premier pike water, Lomond can do even better. It has vast shoals of dace, roach, perch and ruffe, not to mention the unique *powan* in huge numbers. Add to this salmon, trout, sea trout and eels and it becomes a five-star Egon Ronay restaurant for pike. Moreover, the fish-holding areas are far more extensive than in Loch Awe, the whole of the south basin of the loch providing fishing potential as well as certain areas in the north.

The list of impressive fish from Lomond is extensive. The largest in recent years was a 35 lb fish caught by Slim Baxter of Carlisle. Quite a few 30 lb fish have been caught and some argue that a 40-pounder is a real possibility.

Lomond certainly has ample potential. It attracts many visiting anglers from England especially in spring when finding a place to fish can be difficult on the available shoreline. For this reason, I would argue that a boat is essential equipment.

LOCH KEN

Until recently this loch was commercially netted and as a result could always be guaranteed to produce many Jack pike. Now that the netting has stopped, the average size has increased, which augurs well for the future.

The roach shoals in Ken are prolific and, together with a good head of brown trout, a run of game fish and eels, has plenty of potential. Although smaller than Awe or Lomond, virtually the whole of it is a pike-holding area: the average depth is probably no more than 12–15 feet, with deeper areas down to 70. Over the years Ken has produced a number of big fish with the odd authenticated 40-pounder. Ken is, therefore, certainly one to consider in the quest for that elusive big fish.

FORTH AND CLYDE CANAL

Running from Grangemouth in the east to Bowling near Glasgow, the fish-holding potential of this canal is enormous. The population includes perch, pike, roach, tench, bream, carp and trout – and even the odd discarded goldfish has turned up before now. The water is heavily weeded throughout its length, especially in summer but also in winter as a result of recent mild weather.

It warrants a mention both because of its easy accessibility and because it must rank as one of the top coarse fisheries in Scotland. Yet, in all the years that my friends and I have fished these waters, we have struggled. The problem, I believe, is location. Because of its uniform depth there are but few obvious holding areas to try. Some of us launched a determined campaign on the canal some years back and were rewarded with a number of sizeable pike of up to 24 lb. For every successful trip, though, we had to endure a number of blank days. It is not a water for the faint-hearted. Nevertheless, it is certainly one in which the fishing itself is actually easy and one which I would not write off by any means.

TACKLE TIPS

Having given you an idea of where to fish, the next question is what tackle to use. The answer to this one really depends upon how serious you want to take your fishing. What is certain is that you cannot expect to take on fish like pike with inadequate equipment. A fly-rod or match-rod will not be up to the job at all.

My advice for the beginner would be to contact the Pike Anglers Club (details given later). Members will then point you in the direction of suitable tackle shops with proper pike gear. Basic tackle would certainly include:

two 11-foot rods (ask for a 2½ lb test curve – and if the tackle shop doesn't know what you mean, you are in the wrong shop!);

two fixed-spool reels with 15 lb line;

size 6 or 8 treble hooks – the stronger the better;

trace wire, not nylon-covered, of 20 lb strength – a pike's teeth are sharp and will easily bite through nylon;

swivels;

four rod-rests;

a large net;

some form of indicator – which you can buy ready-made, or make yourself from painted table tennis balls;

and, most important of all, a pair of good, large artery forceps – you won't need to perform open-heart surgery but you will want to remove the hooks from Mr Pike without losing your fingers! You are ready to roll.

BAIT

This is simple. A fishmonger can supply you with basics such as mackerel and herring. Aim for smaller-size herring or use the head section or tail section of either herring or mackerel.

You may want to catch bait yourself. Beware, though. When you really need them you can never catch them, so avoid turning up without a supply of bait expecting to catch fresh ones. It doesn't work. Also, take care from where you take them, and remember – trout and salmon parr are obviously out as they are protected. Roach and perch are usually available, but use common sense and do not offend match fishermen by taking fish from their waters.

You can now buy bait from tackle shops. Some stock real herrings in exotic colours, smelt and mackerel. In practice, though, pike tend not to be fussy and every conceivable bait can get results on its day. Remember – pike are scavengers and will feed equally well on dead bait as opposed to live bait. It's handy to have your own freezer as well, especially if your wife doesn't like the idea of smelly vanilla-flavoured mackerel tails sharing freezer space with tomorrow's frozen dinner.

PRESENTATION

You have chosen your water. You have new tackle and a supply of bait. So how do you present it? Again, this can be as complicated as you want to make it.

To my mind the beginner should keep it simple. Free-lined dead baits with proper indication takes some beating. With this method, your line is simply attached via a swivel to your trace to which two treble hooks are already fixed in position. The dead bait is hooked on to the trebles, cast out and rods placed in rests with indicators on the line (note bail arm open).

You then wait for the fish to take the bait. The indicator will drop and line will be taken off the open bail arm. You have a run!

PIKE CONSERVATION

Having successfully caught your fish, the next bit is in my view the most important. You have to unhook it. When looking down the throat of a 20 lb predator like this you realise just what a mean machine the pike really is. It has a dozen or so frontal-gripping teeth; the roof of its mouth and tongue are armed with row upon row of very small teeth all slanted back towards the throat to prevent the prey from escaping. Even the rear edges of the gills are

Mike Maule's pike set-up – note painted table-tennis ball as bite indicator

armed with small teeth. This is where the forceps come in. So too does a tough gardening-type glove to prevent mishaps. Using the forceps, remove the hooks whilst holding the pike still. Again, being in the presence of an experienced pike angler is invaluable. The hooks should then be removed and the fish returned unharmed.

The idea of pike conservation is not that new. Pike have a function as top of the food chain and returning fish alive helps maintain that balance. Furthermore, recognition is now being given to the fact that attempting to remove pike only means that more small pike survive as predation from the bigger ones is reduced. Many waters down south run perfectly well as mixed fisheries of which the pike is recognised as an integral part. Besides, killing a big fish does little to improve the chance of other anglers catching it later on when it might weigh more. There are, therefore, strong arguments to put fish back from both a conservation and a pure angling point of view.

THE PIKE ANGLERS CLUB OF GREAT BRITAIN

This club exists to promote the conservation of pike throughout the country, through a series of regional organisations with a regional organiser (RO) at the helm.

It achieves its objectives by regular local meetings to which both beginners and experienced anglers are welcome. By this informal route experience of how to catch pike, where to fish and how to handle them when caught is gained, not to mention advice given with regard to what tackle to buy and different methods of setting up catching rigs.

I cannot stress strongly enough that anyone contemplating pike angling for the first time should contact his or her local organisation, details of which can be found by contacting the Scottish PAC Secretary at the following address:

Ralston MacPherson
Rosebank, 17 Barrhill Court, Kirkintilloch.

THE PULL OF MULL

Brian Swinbanks

As far back as I can remember, I have been hooked – hooked on Scotland – hooked on fishing. Even in my teens in the '60s the lure of girls took second place to the lure of the river. There was nothing like it. I once got on my scooter, a Lambretta 125, and drove non-stop from Birmingham to the Isle of Mull. I arrived, bow legged and hypothermic, but all I noticed was the river bursting its banks as a massive spate cascaded under the bridge. I knew that the salmon must be running, and I was there to work for a few weeks as the water bailiff and to do some fishing for the Glen Forsa Hotel.

In the hotel kitchen my friend Marie Howitt, the owner, was whipping up the hollandaise sauce and in the sink lay three large silver shapes. I could not wait to get out on the Forsa – I knew every pool, every eddy of that river. And I still go there to fish on my boatman's holiday.

In 1970, when my father died, my mother bought a small hotel in Salen on Mull. She also bought my young brother, Duncan, a 16-foot clinker-built boat which he named *The Rock* – and that was it. We were now hooked on sea angling. Previous trips to Arran had whetted our appetite. Charters out of Brodick with Matthew Laird, where we filled fish boxes with beautiful haddock caught on whole fresh scallops; nights spent on Ayr pier under that unbearable fog-horn fishing for cod and conger – these were all part of our angling education. But Dr Deitrich Burkel of the Department of Natural History at the Glasgow Museum had set our sights on bigger game – the not so 'common' skate. He was convinced that the huge common skate which were being caught at Ullapool, Scrabster, Orkney, and Shetland ranged all over the west coast of Scotland.

We proved him right, catching our first skate from Duncan's dinghy in the Sound of Mull in July 1972 – a monster fish which had eaten a thornback ray, which in turn had eaten our bait! To land it we all leant to one side, rolling the gunnel level with the water. The fish was dragged aboard, dripping and exhausted. Our first skate. We proudly carried it ashore and pushed it home in a wheelbarrow. The 'weigh-in' took place on the human scales outside the local shop. I balanced the huge fish which was draped over two upright fish boxes; Duncan fed pennies into the slot. It weighed 101 lb.

The fish was hung up for the trophy photos. Macho egos satisfied, we all turned for one last look at the fish. My mother, leaning out of an upstairs window, shouted, 'That poor fish looks hideous – cut it down!' My conscience was pricked. Immediately, in conjunction with Duncan and Deitrich Burkel, I formulated a policy for conservation and a philosophy for fishing which I have never regretted. If you are not going to eat it, return it. If it's endangered, *always* return it. For the record, the wings of that first skate were eaten.

The dilemma now, in the 1990s, is to decide which species *are* endangered? Is it the shark or the sand eel? Can we have whales without krill, or swallows without flies? Personally, I wish that we would give more support to the prey and not the predator.

Our fishing expeditions continued throughout that summer. Two more giant skate were caught and released at the side of the dinghy. We also found good shoals of coalfish, pollack and cod. Now I wanted others to share in my experiences, and in June 1974 I gave up my job as a toy designer at Raleigh Industries and started the sea angling charter business, Hebridean Ventures, at Tobermory.

In summer, Tobermory – or Tobar-Mhoire, as it is known in the Gaelic – is the most beautiful harbour on the west coast. A natural amphitheatre of rock surrounds a floating stage of nautical players, the gaily painted shops and houses clinging to the green hillsides. In the winter, fishing boats, yachts and ferries strain at their moorings. Dark dank clouds scurry across the tree line as vicious storms rage out to the west. Mountainous seas engulfing the Cairns of Coll and rolling on towards Ardnamurchan, deposit well-laid creels high up the cliffs, leaving them high and dry when the storm abates, to hang like abseiling mountaineers. Cal Mac's ferry, *Lord of the Isles*, lies secured by a multitude of mooring ropes unable to sail to Tiree. She rises above the pier like a black spider in her web, while aboard, passengers prop up the bar venting their frustration on the optics. The sea-angling boats, the *Amidas*, the *Kittiwake* and the *Laurenca*, moored close inshore, are secure from the full fury of the westerly gales. At last, winter turns to spring, the bay is calm and boats bob on their own reflections. The sound of a power-washer and the smell of paint, resin and varnish hangs over the fishing pier. Another season is upon us, my 16th as a charter skipper.

Sixteen years of fishing, not just as a hobby but getting paid for it. It is every angler's dream – day after day, fish after fish. Loads of cod, coley and pollack. Boxes of haddock and whiting. Thumping, spinning congers, back-breaking skate, clutch-burning runs from tope after tope. Sixteen years, season after season, and never a dull moment.

Hundreds of anglers and thousands of fish have come aboard the *Laurenca*. Scots, English, Dutch, German and French come to fish. Some come in search of the huge elusive skate, others just fish for the pot, like the French angler who insisted on fishing, not with a rod and reel, but with a huge hand-line. The vast wooden frame – like a deck-chair upholstered with string, was carted up to the bows where he sat like some kind of figurehead, occasionally lobbing out a lump of lead to which he had attached a brass wire paternoster more reminiscent of an undernourished Christmas tree decorated with hooks! We were at anchor, and inevitably the strong spring tide forced his tackle through to the stern of the boat, tangling it with other anglers' gear. Quick as a flash, my brother Duncan, being of a mischievous nature, attached the plump codling he had just caught to one of the Frenchman's hooks. Back over the side went the tackle and the cod. After a few seconds there were cries of delight from the bows, 'Ooh là là, skipper! I have caught zee cod.' Time after time small cod and whiting were attached to the Frenchman's line. Sounds of joy and delight filtered down to the stern. At the end of the day he walked up the steps, turned and thanked me for one of the best day's fishing that he had ever had. He never caught a single fish.

The enthusiasm of the continentals for our sport was astonishing. Berty, the Dutch angler from Massluis, was known as the 'walking disaster'. The first year it was his new £500 watch – overboard. The second year, stepping on board for the first time, he tripped, falling face first into the well-deck depositing a case of duty frees. The broken glass, the aroma, the tears. On the third charter we had reached the first mark without mishap. I explained that we would do some light fishing for pollack over the remains of a Cunard liner, now reduced to her boilers and a few buckled plates . Berty produced a new rod – long and light, ideal for pollack. Down into the depths went his bait.

'I have one!' he cried. The rod bent into a circle – he was straining to raise the wreck!

Something had to give and it was not to be a thousand tons of cast iron. The tip of Berty's rod broke off, and then,

A pollack

like falling dominoes, section after section snapped, slowly descending piece by piece down the line. Berty, left holding only the butt section, looked round at the audience – we were in stitches. His forlorn face slowly split into a wide grin. 'O sheet!' he said. 'Berty – walking disaster!', simultaneously throwing the rest of the rod overboard, reel and all!

The exuberance of the Dutch matched their love of the sport, though everything went wrong when it came to hooking big fish. The tope were on the feed – reels screamed in all directions – run after run was missed. Panic and pandemonium are the only words to describe the chaos on board as the Dutch anglers grabbed each other's tackle. They struck in all directions, waving the rods around like conductors' batons.

'Stop!' I shouted. 'Everybody reel in – rebait. If we get any more takes I will hand you the rod and tell you when to strike!' The baits, whole fresh mackerel, went in. Immediately we had a take, the rapid run of a big tope. Grasping the rod with my left hand, I fended off a Dutch angler with my right.

'Let it run – let it run!' I shouted. The reel was screaming, a hundred yards of line disappearing into the ocean. Far below the fish stopped, turned and ran again. I struck and handed Grues his rod. Their first tope – the first of many.

The Dutch were now picking up their own rods and hooking their own fish. We'd had a great day. Dick, the team leader, baited up for the last time. Unfortunately, and without him realising, his bait was tangled with Berty's gear – on the opposite side of the boat. I read the situation.

'Let it run, let it run,' I shouted.

'It's going under the boat,' came the shrill reply.

'Don't panic!' I called. 'Just let it run.'

By now I had his bait, and hook, in my hand on the opposite side of the boat. Two strides and I was across the deck, Dick's rod tip was now under water. The reel stopped screaming as I plunged the hook straight through the back of his billowing waterproof jacket.

'Strike!' I cried down his left ear.

It was like a clip from *Tom and Jerry*. Dick struck and reeled but to no avail – his jacket was stretching, like a sail, out across the deck. His rod bent over the boat's gunnel. We collapsed into a heap as Dick realised that he was fighting himself.

Angling is in the mind. It is all about anticipation – the strike. That magic moment when you are connected by a single strand of nylon to your quarry deep down on the ocean bed. Normally it is just the rattle-rattle of a whiting, or the tug-tug of a cod – sometimes it is the powerful pull of a giant skate. Occasionally all hell breaks loose and a fighting fish of unstoppable power is on. Over the years there have been four such moments.

The first occurred far out, west of Coll, on a hot calm day. The mainland, to the east, shimmered in a blue haze. The Cairns of Coll lifted into the air like blacksmiths' anvils as the heat haze caused the land to mirage above itself. The *Laurenca* wallowed lazily on the oily swells that rolled in – caused by an intense depression far to the south-west and now entering the bay of Biscay. The stern faced the magnificent mountains of Rhum. Through the gap, the Cuillin ridge on Skye was just discernible. The charter party, a group calling themselves the 'Clueless Club' from Liverpool, were jigging and pirking for cod, pollack and coalfish. Good fish – 5–10 lb each – were coming aboard.

Never one to miss an opportunity, I rigged up my rod. The tackle was two red gills (moulded rubber eels) and a huge pirk (a massive cromium-plated metal lure with treble hooks) weighing over a pound. Down, down, down went the pirk, spiralling out of sight into the crystal-clear water. Almost instantly the pirk stopped. I instinctively slid the gear lever forwards. The rod bent over and over and over – I slackened the clutch. Line began to purr off the reel. I tightened the clutch but there was no response from the fish – no head shaking – no 'stop-go'. The fish just headed west and the line had to follow.

Already halfway down the spool, I shouted for the lads to reel in. Colin, who had fished with me many times before, dived into the cabin to start the engine. I shouted instructions.

'Which way, Brian?' he shouted.

'Any flipping way,' came my reply. 'Just turn the key and let's go!'

Colin slammed the throttle full ahead with the boat in gear! He turned the key and the *Laurenca* leapt out of the water like a cart-horse trying to jump a five-barred gate. Simultaneously my spool emptied. The line stretched and parted like a crack of thunder. The huge shark swam on regardless, oblivious to the pandemonium above.

Sharks are exciting, but for some reason I've never been really interested in catching them on the *Laurenca*. If we had put the effort into sharking that we have into skate fishing over the years, who knows? Anglers have had 5 lb cod cut in half by porbeagles. Large sharks, hundreds of

Dusk aboard Laurenca

pounds in weight, have rolled beside the boat as they chased our catches to the surface.

One September Colin MacWean hooked a shark of unbelievable speed and ferocity. We were at anchor fishing for big skate and tope. Colin was on the port side. His bait had hardly touched the bottom when he cried out, 'Skate on!' Seconds later he shouted despondently, 'Lost it.' He started reeling in – then noticed that his line was coming up faster than his rate of retrieve.

'It's still on,' he cried.

'Reel in faster,' I shouted, hoping that he would get in contact with the fish. But the fish had other ideas. Unseen, it veered away, powering out from the port quarter. It broke the surface 30 yards out, did a rapid U-turn and headed straight back towards the boat. As it passed in an arc under the stern, I glimpsed the shimmering silhouette of a huge dark shark. Colin, still trying to gain line on his erratic leviathan, moved rapidly to the transom of the *Laurenca*. He was too late, his frantic efforts to gain control in vain. The shark took off for Ardnamurchan – away from the starboard quarter. With one swipe of its huge tail, the line was smashed. What a fish. Not for one second were we ever fighting that one. The shark was in complete control.

Sharks may be powerful but I would rather land the most exciting and elusive of all our fighting fish – the halibut. Halibut live in the wildest of seas – in areas of intense currents and tide races. Areas like the Pentland Firth. Here underwater peaks and pinnacles cause the surface to boil with turbulence, even on a calm day. The geography of the seabed to the west of Mull reflects the topography of the land. Underwater cliffs and canyons abound – like 'the wall', south of Rhum. Here the seabed falls straight down from 200 to 700 feet. There are underwater hills and pinnacles that rise vertically on their eastern edge (great for pollack), falling gradually away to the west. There are underwater valleys with deep muddy bottoms home to millions of prawns that abound in these food-rich waters.

But when it comes to halibut, my sixth sense homes in on the Cairns of Coll – a series of rocky outcrops rising straight up from the seabed over 250 feet below. The tide races around these exposed and dangerous outcrops as the waters of the Atlantic pour in and out of the Tiree passage. Occasionally, on flat calm days, we anchor here to fish for skate, conger and tope. But I will never forget the day we lost the halibut.

It was early June, a neap tide and a perfect weather forecast. The wake of the *Laurenca* streamed far astern, not a ripple to destroy its line. The turbo whined as 200 horsepower thrust the bows towards the Cairns. Soon we were at anchor on the edge of a deep underwater drop. Down went the big baits, on went the ratchets. The lads then assumed their favourite position for big-game fishing – horizontal, asleep on the deck.

At slack water, Steve Dooley hooked and landed a fantastic 141 lb female skate. Then, just as the tide turned, a bite on Nigel's rod, a run – and what a run! The fish powered off up tide and over the subterranean cliff. As the line sped off the spool at an alarming rate, I frantically tried to drive the boat forwards and take up the anchor rope at the same time. The ABU 10,000 reel was rapidly running out of line. The clutch was unable to arrest the force of the fish. Instinctively, Nigel used his thumb as a brake – very painful. Suddenly the monster fish was off. Nigel reeled in and there, dangling on the end of his line was a small 4 lb ling. Perplexed, I lifted the fish on board. It was covered in small scatches. Unbeknown to me, Nigel had changed from big bait, big hook to a small running ledger rig. The hook was inside the ling. The ling had been inside the halibut. But hook and predator had no chance of meeting! The teeth marks and scratches were those of that elusive big fish.

A shark has an unmistakable signature – massive tears and teeth marks. The skate crushes the bait. Tope leave tiny pin pricks in bands around the mackerel bait. The conger imprints the distinctive V-shape of his jaws on the prey. In British waters no other indigenous fish, apart from a shark, is as strong as a halibut, and this run was back-breaking! Another record lost?

Not all of these titanic battles have failed. August is a good time to fish the 'three mile bank' – aptly named because it is exactly three miles north-west of Ardnamurchan light-house. Ardnamurchan is the most westerly point on the British mainland. The Queen once passed us there aboard the royal yacht *Britannia* with the band of the Coldstream Guards playing on the foredeck. The lads did not know whether to shoulder their rods or carry on fishing. I digress – back to the 'three mile bank' in August. The sea was calm. We were surrounded by beautiful wildlife, guillemots and razorbills ducking and diving deep into the passing shoals of sprats and sand-eels, while shearwaters and gannets wheeled overhead. One gannet, over 100 feet up, folded its wings, and transformed into a yellow-tipped spear. Making minute adjustments to its dive trajectory, it entered the water with suicidal speed – bobbing up a few seconds later with a large mackerel! One gulp, a shake of the tail and the aerial hunter lifted off in its endless search for food.

On the way out a shoal of dolphin had played alongside the boat – shifting back and forth in the bow wave to find the best position, before dropping back to surf in the wake. Occasionally porpoise purposefully finned on the surface. A few minutes later a minke whale, also known as the 'piked' whale or 'lesser rorqual', circled the boat. Over the years this 'fish-eating' whale has been extremely curious about our boat, sometimes circling, occasionally rolling right under the hull. When they blow, upwind of the boat, the pungent fishy aroma is nauseating! Unfortunately, the recent popularity of whales has led to boats chasing them all over the sea in search of better and better photographs. This year no minke whales came alongside our boat; we saw plenty, but they appeared shy. I'd rather wait for them to come to us.

The charter party that day came from Cheshire, Chorley

and the North-east. The sight of such an abundance of wild life was reward enough for these men from the city. But I wanted more – a big skate; a ton-up specimen. Not long after the whale appeared we were rewarded. Colin Stockton hooked a big skate. The battle, a solid struggle between angler and fish, was at stalemate. Colin gained a little line then lost twice as much. Suddenly all hell broke loose. The line powered off up tide and Colin, who had been standing at the stern and facing aft, pirouetted on the spot. The rod, now horizontal, was pointing past the bows. Before Colin could slacken the clutch, the return spring broke, setting the handle in motion like the pedals on a racing bike. I grabbed the rod and told him to go forwards up to the bows. On the *Laurenca* this means climbing out of the well-deck and holding on to the safety rail along the cabin roof before reaching the sanctuary of the pulpit. Colin, a big man, struggled forwards. I followed with the rod, the reel and flailing handle. Now seated on the forward cabin roof, Colin grabbed the rod and arrested the handle. He struck into the monster that was heading for the Cairns of Coll some five miles away. Crack! The line parted! Well, we speculated, we commiserated, we even talked about nuclear submarines. But we had no answer. That was the most powerful run I'd ever seen.

Fifteen minutes later we were into another big skate. The fight was easier this time; the angler was gaining line. But I was worried, for just below the surface there appeared to be a fray in the line.

'Slowly,' I said. 'Slow lift.' Inch by inch the ragged line crept towards the rod tip. I leant over the side. There were two lines, plaited together. The angler stopped reeling as I tried to untwist the second strand of nylon.

Suddenly Colin shouted, 'That's my line!' Not a time to panic – the double blood knot is not easy to tie, especially on a rolling boat. Round and round, one, two, three times, into the centre, hold the end. Now for the other side – round and round. All the time I was praying that the

fish, suspended hundreds of feet below, would not dive. Through the loop in the centre, the knot was now complete.

'Reel in, Colin!' I ordered. A few turns and the weight was on his line – the weight of a big fish! The other angler's tackle spun free. Colin eventually landed the fish, a 110 lb skate which was weighed, photographed, tagged and returned. The only explanation I have for the frantic run involves the whale. Cruising just below the surface, one of the flippers, which stick out at right angles to the body of the whale, must have caught the line. We had been trying to stop a whale – which was pulling a 110 lb skate!

When I first started chartering, I fished all day, every day. I could have been accused of neglecting my clients, but my desire to catch and explore the most distant and exposed marks provided every angler with spectacular sport. Now, the instincts of 'hunter-gatherer' are abating. Today nothing gives me more pleasure than helping a young lad to catch his first mackerel, or a dedicated angler his first skate. Some fishers charter the boat for years before landing their first ton-up fish. Others, like Paul Young, are just born lucky!

When Ricky Walker, director of *Hooked on Scotland*, first approached me – I was apprehensive. There had been programmes about British sea angling before and I had not been impressed. Yes, I had seen some spectacular big-game fishing films, but our fish do not tail walk past the boat at 30 knots. At first, we interviewed each other. Abattoir shots of fish being unceremoniously gaffed and dumped into fish-boxes did not appeal to me. Within a few moments I realised that we were on the same wave-length. Paul and Ricky also cared about fish and conservation.

Historically, May, June and July are the best months for skate fishing at Tobermory. I phoned two of my smaller charter parties and made the arrangements. The crew would join the 'Clueless Club' from Liverpool on the Friday, fish with brother Duncan and I on the Saturday,

Brian Swinbanks on Laurenca

and finally join Tom and Sally Abrahams' party on the Sunday. We also chartered a second boat, the *Adelina*, skippered by Ian Slade, from which the crew could film the action on the *Laurenca*.

The film unit arrived on Thursday, 20 June, and I came ashore at six in the evening, to find them awaiting me: Ricky Walker, producer, Mike Shepley, director, Paul Young – well-known actor and angler, the cameraman Neville and Martin Pollock the underwater cameraman, all his gear. My mind went into overdrive. We already had six anglers plus all their gear on the *Laurenca*. The solution was simple. Ricky and I decided to put all the crew, except for Paul, on the *Adelina*. Paul, doubtful at first, was persuaded. We arranged to meet at eight the next morning.

The film crew, their gear spread all over the pier, were on time. The equipment was soon loaded on board the boats – beautiful new Shimano rods and reels on the *Laurenca*; diving gear, cameras and spare film on the *Adelina*. But where were the lads? Then, swaggering down with all the bravado of a bunch of Everton supporters, came the Liverpool lads, dressed in Bermuda shorts and every stupid hat that they could get their hands on! Peter, sporting a vaguely rude T-shirt, shorts and wellies posed. Within minutes one of them was making a takeover bid for the BBC while the rest tripped over each other in the rush to get in front of the lens! I could not believe it. One of my best groups were behaving like wallies! I left them to it, started the Perkins diesel and we were off!

A slight breeze sprang up as Ardnamurchan lighthouse came abeam. The Bermuda shorts were soon replaced by jeans and the serious business of catching bait began. Bait for skate must be big – and I mean big. It is not uncommon for anglers to use two or even three mackerel on one hook. But my favorite bait is a 'ripe' coalfish. In the early season finding bait can be a problem. Fortunately, the first skate of the season are hungry. Anglers have even caught them on lug worm, sprats, herring, gurnard, whiting and dogfish. A woman angler once landed a 109 lb skate on a set of home-made feathers – unbaited.

For Paul and the Liverpool lads, bait was no problem. We were soon over a vast shoal of coalfish.

'This is a good omen!' I thought, as Neville filmed the action from the *Adelina*. The fishing was fast and furious. Unable to resist, Ricky and Mike Shepley were soon rigged, rods bending into strings of plump coalfish.

Bait aboard, time to anchor. I'd chosen to drop the hook close to the underwater peak over which we had caught the bait. Skate are bottom feeders, favouring areas of gravel and shingle interspersed with rough ridges and boulders, often being found on the top of, or at the base of, underwater cliffs. The tide was ebbing to the south-west. Down went the baits, spiralling diagonally to the seabed 220 feet below.

Paul was fishing on the port side, uptide of the prime positions on the transom. Two of the lads, stretched out on the deck. Others fiddled expectantly with their tackle. Paul was using my new Shimano 4.0 Beastmaster reel and Speedmaster rod, a superbly balanced outfit for big-game fishing. His terminal tackle was a 3-foot trace made from 150 lb breaking-strain stainless-steel wire, a single swivel and a Mustad 10.0 bronze O'Shaugnessy hook. One-and-a-half pounds of lead was clipped to a K. F. Knotless Maxi Boom – ideal for skate-fishing as they can be put on and taken off again without having to cut the line. Every ten minutes we checked the baits. Spur-dog can easily chomp their way through them, hundreds of feet below, with no indication on the rod tip. No bait, no fish. Sure enough, the spurs were on the feed. Baits were checked again and again, traces were untangled and frayed lines replaced. Any spur-dog foolish enough to swallow a massive 10.0 Mustad Seamaster hook was quickly returned to the sea.

The *Adelina* had drifted away down tide. She was too big to anchor in this depth. Suddenly a minke whale erupted from under a cloud of feeding seagulls, its vast body curving out of the water before falling back in a fountain of spray. The gulls wheeled across the sky, then deftly descended on a new shoal of sprats. The whale broached again. I spoke to Ian on the radio. The film crew decided to concentrate on the whale as there was no action on the *Laurenca*. Again and again the whale broached. This spectacular feeding behaviour is a rare sight, but unfortunately the crew never got close enough for really good photos.

The spurs stopped feeding – a sure sign of a big skate below. All was quiet, expectant, in the well-deck of the *Laurenca*. I glanced across at Paul's rod. Slowly, imperceptibly, the tip was curving over. This was visual adrenalin, my senses willing the spool to rotate and the ratchet to sing out. Further over went the tip, click, click, click ran the reel, faster, faster and faster as the line spun away.

'Paul!' I yelled. 'It's a big skate! Hit it – hit it!' Paul picked up the now horizontal rod, struck and the fish was on! I rushed into the cabin and radioed the *Adelina*.

'Skate on!' I shouted down the mike.

Ricky answered. 'Who's got a skate?'

'Paul has!' I replied and then added, 'Seven rods out for skate and Paul has hooked one. Talk about luck.' Nobody could believe it!

The lads immediately rallied round, rapidly reeling in all of their rods. This is not my usual practice. Rods on the opposite side of the boat should be left on the bottom as skate often come on the feed in twos or threes. This fish was vitally important, though. We could not risk a tangle. I helped Paul into his butt-pad and fighting harness. Peter, Irvine and Colin lowered the gantry for weighing. The scales, disgorgers, pliers, gaffs and tagging equipment appeared to order. This was the advantage of fishing with a great crew that knew everything about skate fishing.

Meanwhile, the *Adelina*, whilst on whale watch, had drifted far to the east. Her yellow bulbous bows swung like a compass needle towards the *Laurenca*. A puff of black

smoke belched from her stack as Ian wound up the big
Mercedes diesel. Ten minutes later she was keeping station
a few yards off my port side.

Ricky, grinning from ear to ear, shouted across to Paul,
'What does it feel like?'

'Bloody heavy!' came the reply.

The wind was now freshening from the north-west, but
Neville, camera balanced on his shoulder like the barrel of
a computer-guided tank, just kept on filming! Paul strained
and the mono stretched. Slowly the giant fish was brought
to the surface tantalisingly close to the gaff.

Suddenly it turned and in a fraction of a second the
whole weight of the fish, plus the rippling power of those
massive wings, was heading – crash-diving – back towards
the seabed. The Shimano rod, a compound curve of carbon
and resin, was fully loaded. The line pressed down on
every ring and roller. Paul eased back the clutch and
gradually the 'finished' fish was arrested. Paul laboriously
pumped the skate back to the surface and back to the gaff.
The fish was rapidly weighed, tagged and returned, alive,
to the sea.

Data on the 'tag and release' scheme for common skate
(*Raja batis*) is sent to the Department of Natural History at
Glasgow Museum. Over the past 16 years I have tagged
hundreds and hundreds of these fish – from 14 to 227 lb –
the current British record. Some fish have now been tagged
and released three times, others twice in one day and tags
have even been returned by commercial fishermen from as
far away as Iceland. The majority of fish stay in the same
spot year after year, though.

For those of you who did not see the series, Paul's skate
weighed in at 140 lb. Those who did see the series often
ask, 'Did Paul Young really catch that skate?' Well, the
incredible truth is that he did not only catch a 140 lb skate
but another 60 lb skate the next day!

LAST CASTS

Paul Young

There is no doubting the love and the passion of Scottish anglers for their sport and country, but in these times of great change, we must wonder what the future holds. Fishermen have seen their sport change radically in the last ten or twenty years, so can we be optimistic about its survival as we approach the end of the century?

'Guarded optimism' is the most we may allow ourselves, although some branches of the sport are more at risk than others. The shore and sea angler has perhaps seen sport diminish to the greatest extent. Gone are the numbers of cod, haddock and flatties that made up the most desirable part of the sea angler's catch. Shore fishing is often a lonely and unproductive sport with anglers having to settle for a few coalfish from the beach or some wrasse on the float from rocky promontories. At sea, the same story is told and in many areas the only fish increasing in numbers are dogfish, with spur and lesser spotted making up the bulk of the catch.

If you ask anglers and charter skippers the reason for the dearth of fish, you are most frequently told: 'the boats'. More commercial fishing with attendant diminishing returns and financial pressure on boat owners, means skippers have to work harder to cover costs. With modern

Winter evening on Tweedside

technology, the boats can be extremely efficient fish catch-
ers and if the rules and limits aren't always scrupulously
adhered to, perhaps it is understandable. These fishermen
are making their living, after all, not doing it for fun,
like us.

But perhaps it is time to think in the longer term. Herring
have partially recovered since fishing was curtailed, giving
stocks time to regenerate, but how long will the mackerel
shoals survive the highly efficient exploitation of their
migrations round the British coastline? How long would it
take for the runs of huge Clyde estuary cod to re-establish
themselves? The powers-that-be are well aware that we are
talking about finite resources that need protection. So often
when looking at these problems, my first reaction is wholly
emotional, though the solutions seem distinctly practical.
They are, unfortunately, intensely political, and therefore
not always expedient to enforce.

There are glimmerings of hope. As with Brian Swinbanks,
more anglers are returning fish like tope and skate and in
cases where tagging programmes exist, useful knowledge
of these species is being gained. I'm sure there were mullet
in Scottish estuaries in the past though they seem to have
entered the angling consciousness only recently and I wonder why more of us don't fish for them. Powerful, shy and
not easy to catch, there are substantial numbers round our
coastline providing a test of tackle and technique as does
the bass, another species more commonly found in the
warmer waters of the south of England. Yet bass have
become established from Luce Bay in the extreme south
via the Clyde and Forth estuaries to Dunnet Bay in the
extreme north. Like the mullet, bass is a strong fighter
and a delicious table fish (try it steamed with ginger and
spring onion).

There are, however, some less welcome additions to
resident fish stocks and this time the anglers themselves
are culpable. Coarse fishers using live baits have, over
the years, introduced many new species to Scotland by

emptying their livebait buckets into the water at the end of a day's pike fishing. Dace, rudd and gudgeon have all travelled the long road north this way, but perhaps the most destructive of all is the diminutive ruffe. As if poor old Loch Lomond didn't have enough to cope with in the way of surface vandalism from the power boats and the jet-skiers, the ruffe, or pope, threatens the indigenous populations of trout and powan, and possibly the migratory fish. As well as being yet another competitor for food, the large shoals of ruffe feed voraciously on the eggs and fry of other species and can cause great depredation. Most coarse anglers, however, do care about keeping the balance right and many waters are now carefully nurtured and successful coarse fisheries and the upsurge of interest in Scottish coarse fishing bodes well for the future.

Summer dawn, North Esk

As we have already seen, another non-native fish, the rainbow trout has already changed the face of Scottish angling. Sometimes praised and as often reviled, the rainbow is here to stay. In its rightful place, good sport and fun to fish for, but what about those who escape from their rightful place? Are they, like the ruffe, liable to alter the natural balance? Rainbows are now caught in rivers all over Scotland, sometimes many miles from hatcheries. These fish must migrate, so perhaps we will soon be having runs of sea-going steelheads. We know that rainbows, like ruffe again, are not averse to a breakfast of fry and eggs, so will they displace or even replace the sea trout and affect the numbers of salmon returning to spawn?

The plight of the sea trout is well known. Some famous fisheries are all but bereft of this wonderful sporting fish while others have at least maintained stocks at satisfactory levels. The reasons put forward for the decline are many and varied. Lack of feeding at sea, perhaps connected with commercial sand-eel fishing, and pollution, both industrial and connected with concentrations of salmon farms, have been closely examined. Whatever the causes, much

research has still to be done and we can only hope that
scientists can come up with a solution to ensure that this
fine fish will continue to thrill anglers for generations to
come.

The survival of our most noble fish, the salmon, presents
another, more complicated, picture. Stocks have decreased
dramatically and as with the sea trout, it would seem that
a number of inter-related circumstances are responsible.
Many salmon taken over the last few years have been in
poor condition. This could again be related to the availa-
bility of sand-eels, capelin and other salmon foods which
are now attracting commercial exploitation. On its long
and hazardous migration, the salmon must avoid many
predators but surely the most pernicious is man. Not only
are we vying for many of the creatures salmon feed on, we
are, not always legally, trying to catch them on the high
seas. Baited long lines and miles of monofilament net wait
to intercept them on their way to and from the rivers of
their birth. These rivers in many instances are suffering
from water abstraction and are subject to rapid rises of
coloured water due to the supposed improvements in
drainage of vast areas of hillside, often connected with the
planting of non-native conifers. And surely the imposition
of millions of trees on the Scottish landscape not only
offends the eye, but must alter the quality of the water
draining those plantations and entering our great salmon
rivers.

Certainly man is also trying to improve things for salmon.
Fish are being reared by the million for stocking. Nets
and netting stations have been bought out all round our
coastline and anglers are less likely to kill all fish caught.
On many rivers, strict codes of angling conduct have been
introduced whereby all hen fish caught late in the season
must be returned alive.

With a creature that embodies all the wonderful qualities
of freedom, it has always seemed odd to me that we are
surprised when salmon do not take kindly to being

penned. When bred in cages and artifically fed, there are bound to be genetic changes in a fish used to the wide ocean and foraging for food. Salmon-farming is big business and may have taken some of the pressure off wild fish, but it has put other pressures on them. Escapees join the wild migrating fish and if they interbreed, we do not yet know if the wild fish will be debilitated genetically by the farmed.

It is a tribute to those working for cleaner water that salmon have returned to the once heavily polluted tributaries of the Forth and Clyde and there is cause for cautious optimism. As anglers, we must foster the positive side of salmon conservation and if in some cases this means an imposition of a limit to the number of fish taken from the more prolific beats, then so be it.

Anglers near Eilan Donan Castle

Our native brown trout is also under threat. The fish that was once to be found in almost every burn, river and loch is struggling to survive the ravages of pollution and over-fishing. The lochs of the Highlands and Islands are still the finest places on earth to enjoy angling for wild fish in its finest form, but once prolific rivers like the Tweed, Tay and Don have been overfished to the extent that the greed of one generation of angler has left a barren legacy for the next. The myth that all trout fishing is free for everyone to exploit as they wish should be laid quickly to rest. As with salmon and sea trout, we must put back into our fishing not just what we take out, but more. We must fight for what we believe to be right and support bodies like the Angler's Co-operative Association in their continuing fight for clean and clear water.

Ultimately, the future is in our own hands. If we are not willing to make waves, there may be no water left worth fishing. I believe there are sufficient caring anglers in Scotland to make a collective voice that will be heard above the din of commercialisation and the avarice of the few who would put personal gain above communal natural riches. That richness of flora and fauna is part of Scotland's heritage and we are simply the present guardians for our children. We must not be found wanting.

But then, we anglers are an optimistic bunch. We have to be. Because, without the fishing we would only have the kissing. And that would never do, would it!

NOTES ON CONTRIBUTORS

Ron Greer

Ron is a passionate man, who cut his angling teeth on the Forth and Clyde canal and the Borvie burn. A man who cares deeply about Scotland, its flora and fauna and the right hat to wear according to the weather. His scientific knowledge is beautifully tied in to a deep love of fishing for ferox trout, the distribution of the shoals of ferox bait fish like char, and which hat to wear for which loch. A great fishing companion and fine angler, whichever hat he wears.

Mike Shepley

Architect, town-planner, singer and guitar-player, fine artist, excellent cook, international sea angler, film and video producer, Mike Shepley spends a lot of time fishing all over Scotland then goes to the Middle East and fishes there too. Annoying, isn't it?

Stan Headley

Fellow ex-Scottish National Fly-Fishing Champion, Stan can look from his window to the Loch of Stenness in Orkney. An expert fly tier and thinking angler, his love of fishing Orkney waters for brown trout is evident in the many fine articles he writes for our national angling magazines.

Hughie Smith

A hugely successful saltwater angler, Hughie has represented Scotland over 60 times, both from boat and shore. His attention to detail in bait gathering and keeping is one of the secrets of his success and quite rightly he refuses to tell me any of the others.

Brian Swinbanks

With brother Duncan, Brian is half of tackle manufacturer Bridun, based on Mull. He is also the skipper of that wonderful boat, *Laurenca*, from which so many anglers have had memorable catches. A great enthusiast and fine skipper, Brian lives in Tobermory.

Stan Massey

Perhaps the only world record-holding contributor, Stan's 5 lb 9 oz pollack on 1.5 lb breaking strain nylon holds the IGFA 2 lb-line class Saltwater Fly record. He has also caught a 181 lb skate and an 84 lb Blue Shark on 10 lb line. Annoying, isn't it?

John Kennedy

Captain Kennedy served in the Falklands and being a true fisher, managed to sample the delights of South Atlantic sea trout. He now runs the fishing out of Lochboisdale Hotel, is generous with advice for the visiting angler and an excellent ambassador for South Uist.

Mike Maule

Mike believes Scottish pike are leaner and fitter and fight better than their English counterparts. Originally from England, Mike has seen the light that Scottish men are like their pike and now lives in Edinburgh from where he makes excursions all over Scotland in search of coarse fish.

Jim Brown

A Kirkintilloch tackle dealer, Jim is another Internationalist, having fished for Scotland several times and been Scottish team manager for the World Coarse Fishing Championships in 1981. They were fished near Stratford, England, and Jim tells me there is some great coarse fishing beside the Shakespeare Theatre. A Midsummer-Night's Bream perhaps?

Brian Peterson

Brian represented Scotland nine times in the Fly Fishing International, won the Brown Bowl for the best individual catch at Chew Valley and is now the Scottish team manager. He runs a fishing tackle shop in Greenock, ties a mean fly and in his scarce spare time he fishes in charity competitions to raise money for the needy.

Gerald MacKenzie

Life at Loch Fitty is good for Gerald when people are catching fish, and no one works harder than he to make sure they do. Any good fishery manager must also be a keen fisher and Gerald is both, taking after his dad Iain, one of the Fitty founding fathers. Gerald has also fished for the Scottish Fly Fishing team.

Ricky Walker

For someone who as a lad enjoyed cine photography and fishing, Ricky seems to have landed exactly where he would have wanted. Producing programmes about fishing must be just the job he would have dreamed of. It goes to show that dreams do come true . . . if you work hard enough.